Nick Sanders
Loneliness of the Long Distance Biker

Nick Sanders's Motorcycle Diaries
vol I

by the same author

non-fiction
Journey to the Source of the Nile
22 Days Around the Coast of Britain
The Great Bike Ride
Short Summer in South America
Bicycle: Image and the Dream
Fastest Man Around the World

videos
Longest Narrow Boat Journey in the World
Black Sea Odyssey
Fastest Man Around the World
Kaleidoscope Coast
Journey to the Top of the World
American Dream
Journey to the Edge of the Sahara
4 Go To Europe
The Emerald Way
Road Head
Global Rider Series parts I to IV

DVD's
23 Bikers Around the World
Moto Challenge of Great Britain

Nick Sanders
Loneliness of the Long Distance Biker

On the Road

An **On the Road Book**
P.O. Box 27 Machynlleth Powys SY20 8WT
www.nicksanders.com
www.motochallenge.com

First published in Great Britain by **On the Road Books,** 2004

Set in 10 / 11pt Times New Roman
Layout by Y Lolfa
Jacket by Roger Murray & Rob Nicklen
Jacket photograph by Hugh Brasher
Printed and bound in Great Britain by
Cox & Wyman, Reading

ISBN 0 9549081 0-4

ACKNOWLEDGEMENTS

If it wasn't for the following people this journey would not have happened and I want to thank them all for their trust and support.

THANKS TO:
All the riders who participated in this years Moto Challenge events, to the Challenge crew; Elspeth, Robin and Sue, Terry, Jason, Matt, Steve, Ted and especial thanks to my dear friend Roger Murray. Thanks to Rob at Cyber-space, Paul and Ceri at Ylolfa, Jonathan at Black Mountain. Big thanks to my mates who are always there, to Mike, Martin, Sam and Dom. To the sponsors; Punctureseal, Bennetts, Peter at Webbs in Lincoln and the boys in Peterborough, Jim at Scottleathers, Lloyds Lifestyle, Miles and Libby at Yamaha, Dai and Muerig at HSBC!

Also, as ever to my late and much loved Dad who must be chuckling in his grave. I hope he is still watching over me (but not *all* the time!). And as ever, my ex-wife Hennie, who provided me with useful anecdotal material and three children.

ABOUT THE AUTHOR

Nick Sanders has ridden a motorcycle around the world 5 times so that must make him one the most experienced adventure bikers in the world.

The first time was 38 000 miles on an Enfield 500cc Bullet. The second time was in a record-breaking 31 days 20 hours. The third and forth times were in 2002 when he rode 50 000 miles on a Yamaha R1. One journey was for a TV show, the other when he took 22 riders with him on a 30 000 mile journey; his Motorcycle World Challenge. The fifth time, he took another group on a similar 30 000 mile journey. He has also motorcycled the length of the Americas from Tierra del Fuego to Alaska (30 days). He has led several group expeditions, mostly in North America and North Africa. He has also bicycled around the world twice, the first time in 138 days and the second time in 79 days, setting a new record each time. He has cycled to Timbuktu across the Sahara, cycled the length of South America, cycled along the course of the White Nile and then through 80 countries. He has taken two English canal narrow boats to the Black Sea and back. He is also a microlight pilot and balloonist. Nick Sanders no longer lives with his wife Henrietta because she's had enough of living with him, (who can blame her?) and yes, he has had time to have three children and sometimes lives in Wales.

For Hennie

As soon as one adventure ends, another one begins
Big thanks for the journey *baby*

Prologue

It had taken years for me to summon up the courage to begin writing my autobiography. First I had to wait for my Dad to die, this was something we both agreed. All the rest of my family were dead, and if dysfunctionality was part of the process of my being a child, it wasn't being in the slightest sacrilegious to be thankful that they were no longer alive. Apart from my Dad, of course.

I had intended to write a chapter headed *'How I Got a Sponsor & Set Up The Fastest Man Journey'*. I thought about it for a while, and then I thought differently. Who would be interested in some self centred, conceited d-list celebrity trying to sound important. It was a dry concept and I decided that no one would be interested in such rootless self appraisal. Keeping such content factual might have had merit for an historian, but it risked being dull. Yes, this is autobiographical, but it should be seen as a stage play where characters new and old come and tell me their stories. If I had a choice of a Matisse from which to draw inspiration, or a saucy postcard you buy from the seaside, well, put it this way, in my life story, and remember this well; is that a stick of rock in *yer* pocket boy, or are you just pleased to see me?

Yes, there were the six figure deals, the excruciatingly hard journeys, years away from home; there was unbelievable poverty, near death experiences that became routine and terrible fatigue all linked to a type of ignominy that was sparingly rescued by a blip of occasional fame. My life went very high and very low and my personal life mirrored my job. When my career was good my home life sucked and when the job was down the pan there were times when only my personal life somehow kept me going. There were times when analysis of some of the things I did would have described a man who didn't want to live.

Dullness is just what adventure isn't. It is harder to describe what adventure is, but it's not a parched business. The very air is sweet when a journey is going well. Then, brim full of emotion, adventure carries the sound of twigs that crackle in a desert fire with the smell of mint tea being served. Adventure is not just knowing where you are going but a realisation that *everything* you do is an adventure. In the tradition of Huxley imbibing mescaline to just observe and *be,* Tibetan monks chanting or Sufi's Whirling Dervishes, such thoughts cater for the idea, that *not* going anywhere is also worthy of being called adventure; it is simply part of the distinction between the two main types. One deals precisely with the real *here and now*, the other with the *not* knowing, the *not* being, the *not* doing, and yet, still going out to do it. It describes an incomprehensibleness linked to movement through time and space. Or is it easier to think of it all as some sort of travellers insanity?

The Story

There were so few things I was good at that it makes more interesting reading relating those that eluded me; relationships, being humble, crying, listening, confessing, saying sorry and getting laid regularly until it sort of clicked into place around the time I was 25. Autobiographies are usually not about what you *can't* do, they advertise what you *can* do and who you are, but, the self-defeating nature of the genre, ultimately takes you on a personal journey with someone, and their friends, where you are exposed to their weaknesses as well as their strengths. So you have to start somewhere. A bit like life, you drift into the tale. Has it started? Has it already ended? A note here, a chord there, another note, a word, I was fertile, as are most people?

I mean, the babies, like the journeys, happened without really knowing how. I was just kind of good at it. For several years I turned up at the Motorbike Show in Birmingham, England, where for all to see, my wife bore the weight of my exuberance and had to sit down a lot and be given glasses of water. For years she was always carrying my children. 25 years ago, I set off to bicycle around the world. It wasn't that this first journey was particularly extraordinary; it was the fact that I took only 15 minutes to decide to do it and 10 minutes to pack for it, which separated me from the others. The inspiration was not a long awaited realisation, but a sudden spark of confidence linked to a long held and urgent need to get away from my home life. I didn't need to know where I was going; didn't need to care. All I knew was that I was going. It was like this for me since I started travelling on a bicycle and then a motorbike. I also didn't know if anyone was sufficiently interested in the personal side of what I was doing, and yet after 100 countries and 14 long haul journeys, that was what made it all tick.

Perhaps like other world travellers, the fabric of my thinking was not made up of neat little situations that made sense.

Maybe like all egocentrics, it was a phalanx of rudimentary but interconnecting strands, sampled from the most localised influence to give a simple strength, which compounded the different. Wishing so much that I was quicker of thought, I often wondered what it must be like to be in the mind of a dog. How slow it must be for that mindset to grasp fundamental associations: the tedious life of sparks of understandings that travel slowly across canine synapses. If I could just once experience that, I would be content with the brain that I had. And if I say I felt like trying to understand the life of a dog, I could only say that God knows I've slept with a few, which is as close as I've been to slow thinking.

I know this doesn't make perfect sense, but there is nothing that does. It's not meant to. In contrast to the life that I really wanted, as my journeys somehow multiplied, I had for some time been getting confused and wanted more the life of a simple man. By the time I knew what a simple life was, I'd become too far removed from it to get there. If I still wasn't making my case clear, that's because it just wasn't. One thing I knew, I began to realise that *normal* was not part of my life. Over the years it became more evident that in order to survive and come back, I had to embrace and befriend the battles that take anyone of us to the brink.

Southern Spain, July 2004

I grabbed a few days holiday with my family in the small mountain village of Capileira, which was a sleepy place tucked deeply into the mountains of the Sierra Nevada a little way north east of Granada. This was a place I'd cycled to from Manchester a long time ago. Following Laurie Lee's journey when he wrote his seminal poetry prose book *'As I Stepped Out One Midsummer Morning'*, I flew to Madrid and started riding from there. The main thrust of his journey was that he walked from Vigo in Northern Spain to the southern port of Cadiz via Cordova and Seville. He played his violin and played his part in the civil war, wrote about it, witnessed some of it and mesmerised me. It was 1986 and I'd just bicycled twice around the 4802 mile coast line of Britain. I'd written my own modest little book about it and scuttled off to follow Lee's journey. I bicycled along his route and ended up in Granada late one night. Somehow I ended up in the cities small red light street and a girl jumped out in front of me and just lifted her dress. I was 26 years old and I couldn't believe what I was seeing. She wasn't wearing any knickers, showed me her muff and just laughed and ran off. My Dad would never have believed this. I dared not tell him. He was 80 before one of my girlfriends explained what a lesbian was. In Victorian times of course, they didn't exist, and ladies of the night obviously didn't think that cyclists would spend money frivolously, and how wrong they could be. The next day I cycled over the mountain and descended down the other side. The first village I came to was Capileira.

Twenty years ago the village was quiet, dingy, uninviting and poor. The white walls were unwashed, men were small, and dreary looking old women walked around wearing black. It wasn't as if they were just in mourning for a lost husband - although incredibly for a European country, the civil war had not ended so long before - it was just that they were at a certain age where it was simply time to wear black. Two decades later, I stumbled across the village once again, this time having ridden my wife and two children from England by motorbike and sidecar. The village had progressed 100 years. Such was I taken by what was a revitalised and vibrant community, I decided to live there for part of the year.

That afternoon, in the summer of 2004, I took my children to the beach at Canterran, a little way past Almunacar, a couple of hours down to the coast and then on down a very steep minor road where you could drive onto the beach. It was a naturalist beach and God did I feel *odd*. Every body's dick seemed so, how can I put it, *used* more than mine. But then I was going through a particularly dick-less period. Of course, no one dares admit his or her worst fears but frankly, I didn't give a fig leaf about what anyone was thinking. I hadn't had *relations* with my wife since March and *yeah*, right, something told me that I wasn't alone. Men secretly felt like this, wondering when they were no longer going to *get it*, wishing their dick was bigger, or, more to the point, more *used*. I guess I was only jealous or tediously self pitying. So, for a while, I sat glumly watching my three little children play in the surf; Willow Indian Summer aged 6 and ?, Juno Jupitor age 4 and ? and Tatyana Gazelle aged 2 and a little bit. Just about the time separation of my round the world journeys. Go away, come home, have sex with my wife, go away again. The cycle of life was before me and was surely the real reason why I did what I do. Overwhelmed, as little children are, by their own existence, they were laughing and standing knee high in the sea.

To précis this part of my life I cannot give it a conventional time-line. Chronology is not part of it. Like a concerto that was out of tune, this part of my life only had harmony when listened to at some inconsistent and less than uniform speed. You know when you hear the sound track of a dolphin clucking, well add the complaintive pitch of radio sounds from a far away galaxy and you get an idea how random a travellers mind can generate thought. It could be considered rubbish, or it could be excused for trying to explain a life in a slightly different way.

So, in relating to the events that meant anything in 2004, may I introduce my short-lived sponsorship manager who was an excruciatingly stupid man. He promised me a major deal and turned down the global client who eventually gave me £60k. His mobile phone was stuck to his ear in hotel lobbies and he had eaten far too many free lunches to think clearly. Did he not have a brain between his hair and those lugubrious jowls? I made a note to persuade Mobil for a second think about my *'fastest man'* project and set up a meeting with members of their board. Half the management, their PR people, a girl who brought in the tea were there to listen to me tell them how I wanted to circumnavigate the world overland, faster than it was then thought possible. Whether the record lasted or not was irrelevant because it was the first time it had been attempted. It was the uniqueness of the concept that broke the barriers of what was then, considered unthinkable. The journey catapulted me into motor biking, and for the next 10 years I rode around the world another five times.

The next big thing that curmudgeoned my life to change direction was as usual, a woman. This was the softer side of everything I knew. You see, there was this girl I passed on a boat near Berkhampstead. I was on my way back from the Black Sea. All was going well until I got a tyre stuck around my propeller. The inside cavity was fast around each of the four blades. Nothing like this had ever happened before and as a malfunction, it compares with puncturing both motorbike tyres at the same time. In yet another of my B-movie story-lines, fate was taking me down a route from which I was to learn a great deal and from which, I would be lucky to recover.

In my head I started courting someone who was to become a very unusual wife. Not necessarily in this order; I had my first child; squandered all my money; and drove around in this strange girlfriend's old Ford Cortina, which she claimed she'd driven back from White Russia. I believed anything a nice girl told me. She gave the impression she didn't know what to believe, or at least didn't ask any meaningful questions, so we got married, more or less straightaway. She had no idea I owed the Inland Revenue profits from at least six adventures. Henrietta said I could sleep with the tax inspector if this would reduce my debt, but she was short and fat and I elected to pay the full amount. When all my excuses and protestations of poverty failed, I eventually sent my creditors a cheque from a post office in Death Valley, with a card wishing they were here. I was just a simple man; a youngish adventurer sailing back from the Black Sea with a pair of narrow boats.

The Black Country to Black Sea journey was a heavily sponsored expedition with Wolverhampton and Dudley Breweries. It took several meetings to set up, management were keen and the money was on the table. I also needed somewhere to live, because it was only a matter of time before my then girlfriend would kick me out. She was a world authority on Women in Management studies, and my three years of free therapy was coming to an end.

I raised £100k in four months on a borrowed phone to make sure it was sufficiently capitalised to be successful. Whilst my projects always looked precarious at first, rarely did they not go to plan. When I got back from the journey I was given my marching orders. Three weeks later I met this new girl, and six months later, we decided to marry. Somewhere in between all of this, my dear beloved father died. Dad actually came to the wedding, but in his Cremation Box, and he sat next to Dave, one of my two best men. I remember having a long conversation with the Head Cremator at Dukinfield Crematorium about cremating Dad myself. Farmer Bruce reckoned I'd require two tons of a good hardwood like oak, if a temperature of 1100 degrees were to be raised, which is what would be required to dissipate eight stone of water and two stone of bone, which is what, down from 182 pounds in his stockinged feet, Dad had become. He also got smaller, like me, which should I have wanted to float his pyre across a lake; it would mean the boat would be a less extensive build. The man at the Crematorium told me that it was illegal but didn't know why. I did. The National Forest would have been ravaged by a thousand DIY funeral pyres stretching from Sheffield to Leeds.

The M1 would be in perpetual smoke and motorists would be breathing in generations of deeply loved uncles, until when you hit the M62 and cross the treeless plain, the wood runs out. It happens all the time in India.

However normal I wanted to be, everything I was doing took me away from what I thought I could be. I dreamt often of marrying an air hostess who lived in a *cul de sac*. I went out with one once who worked for Dan Air and it didn't get past the first week. Yet, as much as I strived for normal, normal wasn't what was required to do my job. Normality was a distraction. Normality would have killed me and however hard being different is, at least it meant I wasn't dead.

The Black Sea & The Girl

In between these 12 months, I'd been away for nine. I took my two 62ft long replica working canal boats across the Channel, across Europe and through Serbia during the war. It had been a hard journey down the Danube. I'd sunk one of the boats in 80mph winds, lost everything, craned it back up and started again four days later. I'd sailed past Vukovar in Serbia just after the atrocious bombing, and on the way home, hitch hiked with my 20 tons of rusting steel 3000 miles back to Germany attached to a Romanian push tug called Issacci 9. Add to this my friends the Romanians, their ship-life, the excellent chess players, the backgammon, and the whores whom I always ended up with last after two ships had got in there first. There was also the nervous breakdown, and the jumping into the Danube fully clothed, and so drunk I couldn't think. It was at Regensburg that I'd moored my own boats by the lock, and had been invited to party on a passing cruise boat. I got bored with the company and jumped overboard. I don't remember being naked in a German prison, I do remember the thumping of propellers just feet from where I floated, before the river was closed to shipping. But I was soon unconscious, drifting along the middle of the river only to be picked up 20 kilometres downstream. And why was I in such a state? I had been whoring, and I had gone mad.

In the port of Rousse I moored my boats. Exhausted and having nearly died when I sank one of the boats in 80mph winds, I chased a television interviewer around the harbour shouting protestations of love. "Fuckoff, I won't sleep with you," she shouted, so I walked into town and got more drunk. I wondered from bar to bar in the middle of the night, chatting amiably to anyone who would listen when I decided I wanted a woman. I hailed a cab and he took me to the outskirts of town and deposited me by the front door of a very seedy hotel. I didn't know how bad it was until the morning when I saw the poor and ravaged wasteland. Tin cans and bottles were kicked about by hard youths and the wind stank of sewage. The hotel owner was fat and wore a dirty string vest and demanded my passport before he called for a whore. My room was grimy and there was no shade on the lightbulb and as I lay on my bed I began to sleep, when I was woken up. A woman dressed in a mini-skirt and tights began to crawl all over me. Even though I pushed her away there is a trigger in every man of which he has no control and as soon as she had her hands down my trousers I knew I had lost my battle to stay sane. I had no protection and just before entry, I knew I was playing sexual roulette and should have stopped, but I didn't, and I fucked her.

When I woke in the morning I caught her turning over my pockets but there was nothing there. She screamed at me for more money until the same hotel manager dragged her out to the street and made her get into a taxi. He didn't want any trouble, he didn't want the police. I had no money so walked back across the city to the boats where my small crew were having their breakfast. Oh why wasn't I like everybody else? Why did I suffer so badly from the strains of loneliness, that so deeply were they etched, I risked my life for such crumbs of comfort.

For an hour or more I drifted in the river, barely afloat, just my face above the surface of the water. I don't know why I didn't sink, just that maybe it wasn't my time to die, not yet.

After sailing across Europe and the Channel, I was back in London, passing under Tower Bridge, and in a blur, ended up travelling north along the Grand Union Canal in Northamptonshire. Yep, I was well and truly fucked. And then I met Hennie.

Anyone with a pretty face on a fine pair of legs would have done for me just then. It was obvious to any sensible person that I was not in any fit state to make a considered judgment. For me, anything was better than a Dan Air air hostess, although quite what this girl was about I wasn't quite sure. She said she was a secretary, and when pressed, said she worked in the toilet department at Travis Perkins.

Needless to say I had nothing left when I returned to England. Mentally I was shot to bits. I just wanted everything to end so I could hide away and rest. My Professor girlfriend had chucked me. I still had no money, prospects were untidy and there I was with this girl who wouldn't tell me her family name, and whom I fell in love with at first sight. Of course it couldn't last. I didn't know it then, but a rabbit has more chance of mating with a moose than she had of seeing me into old age, but I didn't care and asked her to marry me anyway.

So, after spending seven hours cutting off that fucking tyre, the one that completely altered the course of my life more than any of my adventures, I set off again on my way home via Berkhampstead from the Romanian port of Galacca.

On the way down to the Black Sea I had strapped my round the world Enfield and sidecar on the tug deck. For all the pomp and circumstance of this being the Rolls Royce of Indian motorcycles, it was, in those days, better off being a fucking anchor than it was a bike, so I lobbed it ashore somewhere in France. So, when I sailed past this girl's short blue narrow boat on the way home from Russia, she was, oddly, waiting for me. She said that she'd been expecting me, even though the curtains she'd hung up were an old spotted dress that she still sometimes liked to wear. This was definitely an odd fish. She actually said without a hint of irony that she knew it was me. So I moored alongside this girl, who living on her boat, said she could look into the future, and let me date her on a month's trial.

Then I rode the length of the Americas with Triumph, and when I got back I got her pregnant. Then I motorcycled around the world in 31 days. I mean, I didn't intend to get her pregnant but I did mean to get the record. Yet isn't that what I'm meant to do? Get records? No, no, the baby thing, that was it. Oh fuck, so that's what we're here for? My Dad thought I was sterile and told the girl that when she first met him. Compared to him I was God's Lothario on earth, but then apart from my mum, and possibly maybe someone called Kitty the rambler, he'd met just after the war, Dad was not what you would call a sex machine.

The pregnant thing was definitely a turning point. Bloody right it was. She thought of running off. She wasn't alone. Yet, that's what I did for a living. I run off. So what was I to do now my Joker card had been played? All those years when I'd got away with it, and bosh, she got me. A new journey was about to begin.

I hadn't seen her for a while. She turned up when I was with my mates in a pub off the canal pond in Little Venice in London. She cut a swathe through my friends, barged past what we were all saying, until she got to me, and looked me in the eye. Everyone backed off and left us to it. The static was too much for any sensible conversation so we went back to my boat and made love.

Two months before this meeting of minds, just before I set off to ride the length of the Americas on a red Triumph 900cc

Daytona - the last model before the T595 - I called her at work and they said she'd left and gone back to Poland. I was gutted. I was equally concerned that Triumph very nearly gave me the T595. They only baulked when management began to appreciate the massive undertaking that was expected from the bike. Very hard riding and not a single malfunction allowed in hundreds of hours and thousands of miles. Not a single component could be allowed to break in a road testing no bike had ever before undergone. The girl was now living with a bloke over in Warsaw and had gone back to him. She was probably wondering if I really was the one to be introduced to her parents over a glass of Chablis. Perhaps not. I remember holding her hand as we went around a roundabout by the Swan Valley service station alongside the Northamptonshire section of the M1; me on my bike, her in her car. Then she disappeared. By the time I'd reached Quito I'd got her out of my system too. At that point I'd ridden down from Buenos Aires to Ushuaia, fallen off and headed north with a broken ankle across the snow-laden Paso de Garibaldi, which was only a few degrees warmer than Cape Horn. I fell off my bike in three inches of snow. I knew it was coming because the front wheel slid three times and I managed to hold it. What on earth possessed me to think that I had the experience to ride in those conditions I do not know. I'd happily chase a pretty girl around a party wearing a blindfold, and still catch her, but I still couldn't ride a bike. On the road, cushioned by the snow, looking up at the moon, in pain, I lay there blinking and then sort of smiled, wondering how I was going to explain to the sponsors that it was all over before I'd got to the start line. All I wanted was a free sports bike and it was preposterous the lengths I was prepared to go to get one. I mean, why didn't I simply go to a dealer and buy one? Oh no, that would have been too easy. Get a job in PR, talk a load of bollocks, earn a stack and buy a bike. Was that too difficult a concept to get into my stupidly progressive head as I lay on the road watching snowflakes drift down from the stars?

I pushed on across Patagonia, and on, the full length of the Pan-American Highway and over the Atacama Desert under a full moon and across Peru in a surreal blaze of dawn and dusk. I heaved and hauled this heavy bike from corner to corner and then down the straights. I cajoled every working part to do my bidding, and mostly it did. This lump of steel and rubber and treasures of machinery helped me traverse Equador at night, *contra les banditos*. When I got back home, having rode from Tierra del Fuego to Alaska in 30 days - I had failed to beat the 19 day car record - I decided as a record attempt it was a disaster and told no one about it, but, as a training run, it had been a success. I was, after all, still alive and even though my ankle was still a bit stiff, my bike riding had improved.

In the rain in the Andes I slept underneath trucks by the side of the road. So utterly and completely disillusioned, that by the Equator, I just wanted to give up and fly home. Deep in Colombia I was pulled off my bike by an angry mob, and it was this which ended the record attempt as I missed my boat to Colon from Cartegena. It was all over. I took my foot off the gas and ambled through Panama and Nicaragua. I skirted El Salvador. I wanted so much to go into the cowboy country and play Russian roulette with my life, but by some fluke of sensible judgment played safe, and instead took back-roads and streambeds across Guatemala and Honduras. I raced across the full length of Mexico to San Antonio. I slept under a table while my bike was being serviced and set off again to ride through the night. I rode and I rode because I didn't know what else to do. Always I had a mission and always I needed some girl's handkerchief attached to my lance.

I was quite simply some fucking manic Don Quixote figure going quietly mad all by myself. Seeking only my own counsel in my helmet for weeks at a time so it was no wonder I was getting good at dealing with loneliness and the absurd. When I returned to my Dad's house, he was there, as always, waiting for me. He was my Mum and my Dad all rolled into one for as long as I can remember. He was the only one who could settle me. He was the only person who gave me unconditional love. "Here's your post son," he would say, because he knew I had to see my mail before we could talk. He chucked me my business post, my junk mail, book clubs, unpaid bills, letters from the Inland Revenue. It was headed unopened for the bin. There were also five letters waiting for me, each franked with a Polish post mark.

I'd forgotten about the girl on the boat. A lot had gone on. A lot of miles. My foot ached. I read each letter and each one wanted me more. A week later she flew back for me and then at a party I got stupid and she ran out saying I was an idiot and I had to lie down in front of her car to stop her leaving, so she reversed. I had just ridden the length of the Americas on a motorbike and who could understand what that does to you, unless you had also done it? A few days later she came back, as she always did, and for a while we lived on my boats and on hers. The job in the toilet department was only temporary. She was actually a model, and had worked in Paris and Berlin, Munich, Tokyo and Milan, but never Sydney or New York. We made love all the way up the Grand Union Canal. There was nothing I could do wrong. We danced naked in the rain, drank champagne and got happily stuck in thick ice at Maida Vale for what seemed like months. Our bubble kept everybody else out and for a brief few weeks we were the bread and butter to each other, the caviar to each others mind. Then slowly it started to happen, once, then twice a week she dumped me. Before long, she only turned up again when she wanted a fuck, which, I must say, would have been churlish to turn down. Where I come from, if a beautiful girl wants to fuck you and then dump you, you don't say no. From where I come from, you buy her another drink, ingratiate yourself, laugh at her jokes, make her feel intelligent and eventually you say thanks, especially if there's a chance you might see her again.

*

At the age of 11, and due to my Dad's bankruptcy, I was forced to move to a council estate in Derbyshire. It was called an *'overspill'* estate and it was for people who have no where else to go and are put where they are told. It wasn't a bad environment but you either win respect or you get thumped. The Hattersley estate was up the road. This was where child killer Myra Hindley had lived, and the boys from there would come down to Gamesley where I spent my teenage years, and all hell would kick off. The people from the nearby town of Glossop hated us, and I can't say I blamed them. 4000 people from the squit end of Manchester descended onto a local community, and in the early days as I was growing up, it was a social disaster. As an 11 year old, kicked out of my family home and rejected by my local environment, I reckoned that either I stayed put, or I peeked over the fence. Once I saw what there was to see, another fence. I soon realised that I had to jump over a lot of fences, I had to do more than that, I had to learn how to move through time and space.

"Cup of tea?" said Dad.

"Go on then," I said to him softly. Letters in my hand. He was nearly deaf, going blind, didn't care a tuppence. Humility strapped across his chest like an anchor. Modest to the point of invisibility. Yet he made a cracking cuppa. Always warmed the cup, never a mug, 1 and ? teaspoonfuls of sugar, a delicate infusion and just enough tea to the brim to be polite.

"So what was your journey like this time," he said, "the usual?"

"More or less Dad, you know what its like," and I stirred my tea, quietly contemplating my letters from this girl. I didn't know it then, but she would be with me when I took 19 Triumph riders to Alaska for what was the longest ever tour, that until then, had been attempted. She was to stay with me whilst I rode around the world on a Triumph Daytona and twice around the world on a Yamaha R1. She saw the tail end of a journey by boat from Russia, and another motorbike ride the longitudinal length of the planet from the Uttermost Ends of the Earth to the Top of the World. She was there when my Dad was taken ill the first time. Then there were the babies that slipped into my hands like eels. It was a lot to live for and equally a lot to leave behind. Then I said something odd. "Dad, did you know that I'd actually been away, going around the world, because when I went to Katmandu for three months you were always in the pub and you said you didn't know I'd gone." He didn't say anything and I wondered if he'd heard. Having only ever travelled to Paris for a long weekend after the war, he was the last person you'd expect to understand me, but he saw it all in my eyes.

"Son," he said gravely, "when you leave this house I'm with you every inch of the way. Every thought you've had I've thought it through for you. Every sadness, I've been sad for you, every moment of happiness I've tried to share in my dreams. I couldn't be there with you, but my spirit followed you everywhere you went." He then got up to go to bed. I marveled at the way my father cared for me. As a 37-year-old man, he held me in his head like a child. Still, I hung on to those letters real tight, for a few months later he would be dead.

*

I had to leave London. I was trying to prepare to ride around the world in less than 33 days and beat the car record. My sponsors, Mobil, Triumph and IBM, knew I needed time to get my head together. Physically I was fine but my this girl had put my head into a mess. So the cottage I moved to in Derbyshire was kind of going back to my roots. I tried to lease an office in the town but it didn't work out. It was getting really mad. I couldn't put my finger on it but if I think back, Hennie and I were both bouncing around a nucleus of bedlam. I'd begun to talk to editors in the motoring magazines about possibly taking a car around the world, maybe in 12 days. After a brief introduction at the Mobil garden party with the McLaren boss, Ron Dennis, we had several further conversations about operating this journey with his F1 production car. We got as far as positioning two professional drivers with me, possible a well known ex F1 driver. I was just putting the feelers out for what might make a good story, when suddenly; she jumped on a National Express bus to Stockport, and asked me to pick her up. The moment she got off she showed me one of her breasts and squeezed her nipple, which produced a blob of watery but allegedly highly nutritious milk, and what was I going to do about it? Do what? I remember leaving that pub in Maida Vale and going back to my boat. I remember being 50% responsible for the consummation of life but had no idea where we went from there. Secretly, the fact that this girl was going to have my baby gave me a warm feeling. It allowed me to think that life goes on. It consolidated the notion that the interminable conveyor belt of life, whilst endless, had allowed me a foothold. That this girl, who was carrying my baby, had fulfilled the greatest of my dreams.

*

I'd known for a long time that in my way of life, maybe on the fringe of show business, you are only as good as your last show. I reckoned that offering around the world motorcycling a slightly funkier image was a lot fun, even though I didn't know that then. I had no real knowledge of the mindset of bikers, many of whom deeply believed that riding their bike was one of the most important things in their life. That is the cool thing about biking. So, there I was, entering the greatest dichotomy of my life: going around the world on a great bike quickly and getting paid for it, and becoming a daddy for the very first time.

A Visit to My Sponsors, March 2004

I caught the train to Weybridge in Surrey for my meeting with Yamaha. After being with them for three years we were beginning to feel comfortable with each other. Of course I wasn't Valentino Rossi, but everyone holds a piece of the jigsaw in his hands. Yamaha's fair attitude to me completely secured my loyalty. UK Sales Director Miles Taylor's quiet and interested attention to my plans was all I needed and at the modest level that I was operating, life was not about how much money was available. Financial life at my level had a lot to do with respect. A genuine desire to be understood about what I was trying to do was as important to me as a cheque. Always before I meet Miles, I sneak into the back to see the factory mechanics, of which George most often worked on my bikes. These guys were so important to me prior to me setting up my own machine after which I had insisted no one rides it in except me. It has been a rule of mine never to let anyone ride my bike. As soon as it gets known that my 2004 R1 was available for a quick spin, it becomes little more than a demonstrator, as its balls would get rattled like castanets the moment I was out of sight. When the time came, later in the year, to ride around the world, I would want to know that every mechanical element had been ridden well, each component and part taken to speed in exactly the right way. If I had a back up crew then it wouldn't matter, but much of my riding is away from workshops capable of dealing with such an engine so I rarely rode it in anger and only occasionally close to it's maximum stress level.

I'd been talking to Yamaha ever since my association with Triumph ended in 2001. Author and ex editor of Bike magazine Hugo Wilson, was one of my first contacts in the bike world and at the 2000 MCI bike show in Birmingham, he took me up to the Yamaha stand and introduced me to one of the Yamaha management team, Martin Marshall. Martin had the ear of the then National Sales Director Dan Harris who was, on all of our meetings, a very sympathetic man. Dan quickly agreed in principle to supporting me and it was a blow when he moved to the editorship of Fast Bike magazine, and doubly so when Martin also moved on. Miles Taylor took over both jobs and whilst he was known to be fair, he was a very busy man and we were an unknown entity to each other. It was clear that I almost had to start the negotiations over again. I'd managed to secure a pit lane pass for the 2001 Moto GP at Donnington Park and wondered around the hospitality areas of the big teams. Part of the deal is being seen in the right places, and there was nowhere better than here at the most prestigious event of the season. Testament to the importance of the occasion was when Valentino Rossi rode past me on a small scooter as I was chatting to Martin, and it struck me then, that in a true meritocracy, you get rewarded according not to the size of your talent, but how effectively your talent fits into the market needs. A film producer guy I'd recently met was trying to make an introduction for me to Red Bull. I met the film guy a couple of times later and we arranged to meet up when I was next in LA. His intended film about GP racing didn't materialise and neither did his friendship. I remember calling him when on the outskirts of Santa Barbara, where he lived and he'd conveniently forgotten who I was. The business side of PR, with those necessary introductions were fickle. When I once met Alexie Sayle at a function, I spoke to him about this and he was abrupt when he said that 'if you can't stand the heat, you get out of the kitchen.' How right he was, and years on I was still in the chip fat, frying.

Eventually I closed the deal with Miles and rode the 2001 R1 around the world twice the following year with consummate ease. I didn't know if I registered in the Japanese mindset back at their headquarters in Shizuoka, but bikes are not given away often in the industry. When I spoke to a Yamaha dealer in Perth, Western Australia, who'd been with the company for 30 years, he gave me assurances that the Japanese didn't miss a trick. If an R1 is taken around the world for the first time in its glorious history, then it's noted. If this is repeated in the same year and becomes a double is highly noted. The notional idea that it could be capable of such a feat, was rubber-stamped by my having done it not once, but twice. The fact that I had plans to do it a third and forth time was beyond their imagination and would dispel the myth that this classic super sports bike of all time, was not a suitable machine on which to ride long distances.

*

In 1999 I received an unsolicited email from Clement Salvadori informing me almost rhetorically that 'did I realize my 28 day 12 000 mile Top of the World Expedition to Alaska was the longest ever group tour yet to be organised?' I hadn't given it much thought because as usual the idea came about through pure financial need rather than a need for notoriety. One early summer when I was having a couple of weeks rest at my mother-in-laws house near Benissa by the Costa del Blanco, I hatched the plan with Hennie to take up to 20 Triumph riders across a little known route called the 'Top of the World Highway'. I couldn't believe my luck when I saw it on the map and although it would take us barely a morning to ride it, it would take us seven days to get there from New York. As a concept it reminded me of Lucas-Bridges book *'Uttermost Ends of the Earth'* which described his white ancestors settling in Tierra del Fuego alongside the Haush, Ona, Yahgan and Alacaluf Indians. The perfectly logical polarity was not lost on me, but Alaska was easier to get to with a group. Clement brought the size of the project into focus and as a result I made a mental note to get in touch should the need arise. As well as being a noted motorcycle author and journalist, he had also ridden around the world as a younger man, and there was a long standing invite to visit when near his home, spitting distance from Big Sur in northern California.

*

The Scottish Bike Show, March 2004

When your head is full of the sands of the Sahara or some other God forsaken void, like having stepped off a fast ride, it takes a little while to relax. So when I ended up at Peter Mackintyre's house, which was about to change. Peter, boss of Highland Rider, takes less experienced riders on gentle tours around Scotland and is one of the most charismatic men in the touring business. The last time I was at the Scottish Bike Show he invited me to stay at his house, got me drunk and preceded to try and inveigle me out of my takings from selling my videos. "C'mon, double or quits yer English Sassenach bastard," he shouted, lurching around his armchair. Roddy and big Jim were there to watch over me and his pretty wife had by now gone to bed. I told him that the only reason his wife stayed with him was because of his money and he agreed, but then he was a very agreeable man. He usually agreed with everything I said only because of the unadulterated cheek I gave him. Peter started fishing, as a boy off the west coast and in time became one of the biggest distributors of fresh fish in Scotland. He said he didn't know how much he was worth and Roddy concurred with the view that wealthy Scots don't know what they have in the bank. The more they have, the more they don't know. "C'mon yer bastard, get yer money out!" I'd made two thousand pounds and it was already on the table but Roddy made me put it away and told Peter to get a grip on himself, but having consumed a bottle of Bushmills, which was now percolating through the lining of his stomach, this was increasingly becoming harder to do. By the time he'd drunk a final glass before bedtime, his cavalier spirit was now buried in a coach full of cushions and my winnings still belonged to me. "Once you'd started betting with Peter," Roddy said to me, "he wouldn't have stopped until he'd won your house, and that's no lie."

The next day was the second and last day of the show and around lunchtime I bumped into Jim Aird, boss of Scottleathers. Jim made me my leathers when I rode around the coast of British on my T595 and ran his self-owned family business in the way an independent worked against the giants. I was connected with Hein Gericke at the time but it was sensible not to keep all of one's eggs in the proverbial basket, and in any case, Jim and I got on really well and had the same sort of relationship I enjoyed in the early days with Gericke boss Guy Mainwaring. Nothing materialised with that meeting and it wasn't until early summer that I was to call on Jim again. Much of motorcycle sponsorship was small beer compared to the larger investments made with me by companies operating on a broader PR profile. But a niche market where everyone knows you, and buys from you, is very important indeed. I enjoyed the attention I received from my motorcycling audience, but I respected the need to nurture it like a growing plant and made sure it was cared for.

Wales & Ireland, April 2004

For days, the digger worked on my land to create space for tented accommodation for up to 80 riders. By the time Gareth had finished, the overall effect made my grounds look more like a shit hole than ever. It wasn't his fault, he did a fine job, but there was too much rock and I felt I was living in a quarry. On account of eight tones of testosterone arriving to drink beer and talk about women (and do a bit of biking), the family had scampered off to hide in the hills for the weekend. My 'Open Day' was intended to kick start the Moto Challenge season of events, the first one being the Moto Challenge of Wales and Ireland and the following week a small contingent of riders rode with me to Holyhead to ride around Ireland.

The last time I sailed on the HFC ferry from Holyhead to Dun Laoghaire it was on the bridge with an old mate, Captain Simon Mills. He let me manoeuvre the ship, adjusting the position of the massive turbine jets, which spewed out 32 tons of water a minute, or maybe it was every second. The joystick, which steered the ship, was a little bigger than my hand. I thought I was steering in a straight line but when I looked behind I had zigzagged this 20 000 ton vessel for nearly a mile, and if anyone on board had noticed, they would have thought the Captain pissed – which Simon sometimes was, but never at work. The owner of a number of bikes, a great Ducati man, it would have been good to chat again, but due to a damaged water pipe, the fast ferry was delayed so we took the slow one instead.

Once we were off loaded, one of the riders, a man who lived in France but local to Dublin, led us across the city, south west to County Meath where I suggested we all meet at Morrisseys, one of Irelands most unusual and famous pubs. I stayed on whilst the others rode to the hostel for the night and sat outside on a bench just thinking about life and my travels.

My grandmother was Irish and I think so was my mother. Born in Limerick they were desperately poor. What I know about my family history you could write on a postcard. There was no illustrious lineage and little character interest, but they were a solid body of small unimaginative merchants and shopkeepers that could make money, but hadn't got the brains to keep it. In my family the first generation made the money, the second drank it and pissed it out the pub door and here I am, in penury, trying to make it again. As the journey continued south to Cove and then over to the west coast where the sea laps at the shores of Ireland and America, we all made it to Kate Kearneys Cottage at the northern face of the Gap of Dunloe. Greg sat down at my table and looked at me long and hard. As he sat down, his big belly had made him breathless. "I'll be honest with you Nick, you're a nice guy, but the only decision I want to make during my holiday is to decide the size of my Gin and Tonic!" What a great one liner! I smiled. Had to hand it to the man, he wasn't afraid to cut me down to the quick. I wanted to say *'so what the hell are you doing here then?'* But I didn't. I sat there meekly, nodding in agreement like those plastic dogs you see in the rear windows of Ford Mondeos, where the head is loosely jointed to the rest of their body. At that moment I felt as if my reason for being on this trip was a big mistake. No one should have invited me on the tour I had purportedly organised. Greg gave me the impression that a drinks trolley would have made a better tour guide than me.

"Yes, I know what you mean," I said, but I didn't really. Greg had retired from his business which had turned over seven million pounds each year and employed 73 people. He was at the top of his tree, something to do with outdoor amenities. He was a better businessman than I would ever be, but I did wonder about the holistic view, whereby if he drank less gin and lost six stone he might enjoy his retirement without getting out of breath. Although, as a customer, he was certainly more than entitled to an easier time than having to deal with the dysfunction I cheerfully called an organised tour. The only thing organised about this trip was that it had a beginning, an end, and a journey of your choice in between. It was this *choice in between* that compromised his drinking habits and I wasn't sure which of the two clouded his view, but it certainly wasn't the same as mine. Yet, by the end of the trip he was still smiling, more I think because he was leaving, and could resume a life centred around his cocktail cabinet and ice dispensing machine, which no doubt graced a very large living room. One of my world riders once said to me, that the only difference between being poor and being rich, is that when you have money, you sit further away from a larger TV.

When I was last standing on the top of the Cliffs of Mohar it was winter and I was alone. I was riding one of Jim d'Arcy's sidecars attached to a Triumph Thunderbird. Filming a TV show called 'Emerald Way' I had to shoot three programmes in nine days, of which eight were wet. The dry day occurred when I rode here and into Doolin, and the fragments of sunshine turned this part of Ireland into God's own country. I searched for characters to interview and heard about a recently deceased local sheep farmer who ended up playing his fiddle at Carnegie Hall in New York. I stood outside his house where he and his brother lived, violin virtuosos, looking out across the Atlantic, which lapped against this area of bog, as well as Manhattan.

Amongst the many wonderful people I have met, he and Robert Fulton were ones that got away. When I set off on my 31 day journey in 1997, my operative at IBM had set up a meeting with Mr Fulton, who was probably the oldest man still alive to have to ridden around the world. Then there was me, simply the latest circumnavigator, albeit aiming to be the quickest. Typically, I didn't have time to meet him. Two years later when I started filming *'Global Rider'*, I called his family in Connecticut to try and arrange a short film shoot, but once again it didn't happen. It was February in New York State and he wasn't feeling well enough to receive visitors. The next time I heard about him was in early 2004, when I read, with great sadness, his obituary in the Times.

This time round I caught up with my friend Robin Gregory, who was the Sergeant Major of all my guides. The Cliffs were besieged by hundreds of coach trippers, they had a perfect right to be there but it was too much for me, so I suggested we split and have a coffee at a small music café I knew in Doolin itself. A guy from Prague owned the place and ran it with a pretty but haughty Irish girl. We sat quietly for a while, just soaking up our time off the bike. Robin rides fast and smooth and all the riders respect his skill. With me he rides more moderately. We are the guides, so when we can, we take the foot off the gas. I've followed him and marvelled at his clean clear riding style. He is definitely quick and while he can be passed, his technique is awesome. He rides his heart out, and when you consider that just a few years ago he endured a quadruple heart by-pass, this could be taken in a literal sense. It got to a point when he could hardly walk up the stairs to his bedroom. So incapacitated had he become, that he needed a rest after walking 20 paces. I lost my heart in San Francisco is a soliloquy written for Robin, except for him it was somewhere like Blackpool. Now he was a different man and what a rider. The man is 100% enthusiastic about motor biking and shagging his wife. No one I know puts such energy and commitment into his motorcycling or his sex life. He swims along small lanes like in eel in water. Also, because of his health he simply cannot afford to fall. We continued to sip our coffee, clearly over staying our allotted rest time, knowing we still had to speed over the hard limestone crags of the Burran.

We rode hard to Malin Head and then over the top road until we reached the start of the Antrim Coast. The Causeway was also busy with tourists, Cormorants and Razerbills. There was a bench on which people were seated and next to this there was a narrow gap. This gap was like a door, or could be thought of as a portal into another world. When you looked through it you had a view of an amphitheatre with hugely high sides. From sea to sky the basalt rock was abrupt and magnificent. The sense of being closed in was all too obvious. There was also the thought that these columns of rapidly cooled volcanic rock were watching you. There was a feeling that sent a shiver down my spine which made me feel that this stone knew who you were, that apart from a small stitch of time, you were part of them, bones to bones, all of us ultimately ignominious fossils that compact to dynastic cathedrals of cretaceous rock.

Spooky though it was, I reckon it would have been great to camp here, but only if your head was happy enough to ward off the dark souls. Dave, Carl, Martin and Robin hung around waiting for the bus ride back up to the visitor centre. Easy going, resourceful, calm, they were the perfect travelling companions, especially Dave. He had signed up to ride around the world with me and he'd need to be all of this. Robin was kind of getting used to how I ran things, but then so was I.

After a run in the rain we crossed Northern Ireland to Belfast. Once installed into our hostel in Belfast I looked out of my window where I was high enough to see over the rooftops. Below at street level, a group of elderly men were talking into a small portable sound system. They spoke about how God's Son took on the sins of the world, and how He died to save us. Well He must have been looking after us on the run in from Bushmill. The rain bucketed down in dirty great droplets. The route, whilst not the notorious Skerries, had a rippled surface which at speed pinged the sports bikes into the air for 15% of the time. The guys on the heavier machines sat like bisons and budged not one bit. The spray from the cars spread-sheeted across the road and several of us had tyres as bald as a coot and we all wondered when we might aquaplane. My visor was scratched and old and didn't allow me a clear view. A Moto Guzzi sped past me nimbly with its characteristic rumble. Time and again, this journey around Ireland pushed us all to ride better technically. The small roads in the west were a warren of small uneven surfaces, bumps that could derail a finely tuned sports bike with only a lightweight man on a slender mechanical frame to firm it onto the ground.

Europe, May 2004

Jonathon, the boss at the Black Mountain Yamaha dealership in Abervagenny was giving my bike a quick 7000 mile service before later that afternoon, I started the Moto Challenge of Europe. I'd had the bike three weeks and so far there was nothing about its handling capabilities that I could criticise. I suppose its lightness was a factor in losing traction at high speed on the rippled west coast roads of Ireland. The back tyre was off the ground more than I liked, especially when the tyre is so close to the wire. The thrill of riding such a bike, any bike, is total. You govern where you wish to be in space and time. With a flip of the wrist you are there. With a shift of balance you have rounded a bend, overtaken anything that moves on the road and stopped in a second, the moment you wanted to get off. After a quick oil change, Mark cleaned out the air filter and blew out the remnants of sand that remained since I'd journeyed to Morocco in April. Soon I was away once again.

The days before an event are always nerve-wracking. It's good not to be complacent and my time in the office was spent sorting out the final detail. I'd been waiting for faxed confirmation from overseas campsites but because an incorrect fax number had been sent out, no one could get back to me. There were a lot of holes in the planning which I still had to plug. Campsites were eventually contacted and booked, the Nurburgring people were aware of us wanting to ride on the track. Robin was in charge of the routing and production of the handbook whilst I concentrated more with the basic logistics of getting people and bikes to Spain. The ferry from Portsmouth to Bilbao had at last been booked after several conversations with Tricia Dixon at P & O. "There are two Tricia's in the office," she said, "but if you ask for Tricia Dixon M-B-*Eeeee*, you'll get to me."

"How did you get that?" I asked.

"Well my husband was a Commodore and I got it for services to my husband." Gosh, Trish, I didn't think you got one for that, I nearly said, but instead had her confirm we had 30 riders, a van and a crew of four booked on the boat and left it at that.

By evening I'd picked up Elspeth from her home, a converted water tower in Surrey. She was an incredible woman and a fantastic supporter of what I was trying to do and would crew for me whenever she could. She possessed a warm heart and was a special friend. We drove to meet the riders at the BMF Rally at some hop farm in Kent and the next day we made Portsmouth, loaded everyone onto the boat, and after dumping my stuff in my cabin, I sat quietly in a Brasserie, listening to the pianist. I was sullen because for a while I felt it was all going wrong. The Moto Challenge concept of fusing touring with racing was a good one, but I didn't always feel competent at what I did. So many small elements had to be tightened and the detail didn't come easily to me. My European guide, and world rider Marco, upset my quiet thoughts when he burst in on me and said that one of the customers, big Scottish Bob, was looking for me. He said that he had found a woman in the ship who wanted to come along with him and was that alright? Given that there was probably a paucity of women in Thurso, where he lived, who'd shag him, I reckoned that was what he was here for, and it was fine by me. When I met the other riders from Thurso and Perthshire, they reckoned he'd be burning rubber. They laughed. Big Bob was clearly one of life's big characters.

When the boat docked at Bilbao, Big Bob was nowhere to be seen. He was last spotted polishing off his twentieth whisky with a woman lolling on his knee, nearly asleep, and this morning someone said he wasn't feeling well. An hour from Bilbao we turned off the autoroute and descended south into the Picos de Europa. Moments later there was a near fatal accident. Essex boy Jason crashed after the village of Panes by the head of a gorge known locally as *Desfiladero de la Hermida*. First hand reports had him taking a right-hander too wide. He crossed the white line, clipped an oncoming car by puncturing the front left tyre with his clutch casing instantly shoving the wheel back into the arch. Scraping down the driver side, he skedaddled into the right hand gorge wall and in a shower of sparks eventually came to a standstill. The clutch cover on his bike was pierced and the oil pipe had burst. He was covered in hot oil and as we all arrived, we also found the driver of the car shaking like a leaf. Another couple of inches to the left and either Jason would have flown threw the windscreen and maybe out via the back window - perhaps a leg might have left separately by a side door - or maybe as a stand in for Superman he would have flown over the bonnet and into the gorge. "I stayed upright Nick, *dinn I*," he said, "I mean, I managed to keep the bike under control; I *fort-tit* and I *fink* I did quite well. What do you *fink* Nick?" Quite! Hello RAC Rescue, goodbye Jason. £500 for a boat ride and an hour on the bike is an expensive way to ride your motorcycle and we never saw him again.

At the Puerto del Pontin we turned left up a track hidden between cow sheds that ordinarily would never be found by a motorist. There we climbed and for 30 minutes we started to become eagles, counter steering into corners in the way birds tilt the tips of their wings. When we arrived at our hotel stop at Estrella Lizarra, more riders' tales began to unearth. A guy called Dave dropped his bike, as did Paul. As we were all having dinner in a nearby restaurant, someone calls Elspeth and she then hands me the phone. It's Jason; "I'm on my way mate. I got to a dealer in Santander and persuaded him to fix my oil pipe and it won't be long now. I'll ring you when I'm nearer." Good lad. He was looking after himself, admirably taking responsibility for his unfortunate riding habits. Then Ian from Thurso called, he had finally made it to Logrono about 15 miles away but couldn't ride a moment longer. Lord bless these boys because it's only their first day. Ian reckoned that, a day into the trip, and he might have to go home. I was still on my prawn salad starter when my mobile then rang, "er, me oil pipe has burst again Nick, causing a motorist behind me to slide and crash into a motorway barrier – 'er, the police 'ave been called and I *fink* it'll take a bit longer to get to you – 'er, where are you tomorrow?"

The next day, Elspeth called Ian but we'd have lost contact. *'Earth to Mars, this is a motorcycle tour and we are now approaching day 2 with trepidation. Do we have contact, but no, he's gone again'.*

The next day we reached the Pyrenees. At lunch, after the dirt track short cut, the riders passed another of those awfully dangerous gorges where you take off your helmet and hurl yourself into a riverbed. I got a call from Dave Marsden that Paul Barker had come off, that his bike is a wreck. He crashed 6ft away from a ravine and the machine – a Randy Mamola Special Edition BMW Boxer Cub – ended up being pulled out of a stream by a tractor. What happened to him? I said to Robin that apart from saving on hotel bills, if we carried on like this they'll be nobody left. "Is it normal," I asked him, "for riders to bin their bikes with such apparent insouciance?" Robin's eyebrows met his hairline and he looked up to the sky.

Then there was the fast ride to Perpignon against Matt and Dave. I preferred to ride alone incase someone, perhaps in a friendly gesture, threw themselves in front of me. Nervously, I rode damn hard when I saw them approach from behind; cornering between the bushes of yellow gorse around the bowl of hills surrounding Quillian. Past the canyon there were long straights where I decided to see what an R1 could do. I dangled them for a minute, and whoosh, I was gone.

To their surprise I caught Chris and Lorna on their Blade, and we stopped to have a beer at the Café de la Posts in the centre of Perpignion. It took ages to find the campsite at Le Bacares and past midnight, the Scots eventually turned up. It was Mandy's honeymoon and we hadn't seen them for two days and they were very displeased. I bought Mandy a pint and that cheered her up, but Ian had gone for good.

My Wife is Betty Blue

It's a Wednesday and I am on my way to Antibes. I couldn't find the little road on the seaside of the etang so rode inland on the N112. I stopped by a beach hut, which was like a stage prop from the film set of Betty Blue where the wonderfully sexy Beatrice Dalle played the headline character.

I ordered a cheese and ham panini and sat back watching life parade before me. My phone rang. I expected to hear about more riders trashing their bikes. My Betty Blue beach hut had become my office as I took a series of calls, when my mobile rang once again. I just didn't want to answer it. If any more bikes were to go down this would turn into Moto Challenge Hospital Ride and we'd need George Clooney from ER to guide instead of me, so reluctantly I opened the line. It was my wife Hennie. It was always so nice to hear from her, except she hadn't much to say other than she wanted a divorce. I didn't say much, just looked around and watched people play happy families with their children. Why bother telling me on the phone when a fax would have done. It struck me as weird to think that one-minute everything was OK and the next it wasn't. I remember making love to my wife believing it was beautiful (obviously an over simplification), when the very next day she said, in a matter of fact way, that it was all over. That bland consistency of emotion is necessary to terminate a relationship, but equally it was usually attached to the kind of sex you pay for. I was Zorg, and in the synopsis of the film, Henrietta played Dalle. It concerns him playing a handyman working in France, looking after a collection of beach huts. Working diligently and writing in his spare time, all is well until one day Betty walks into his life. This is a young woman who is as wild and unpredictable as she is beautiful. Slowly, Betty's wild habits and actions begin to become awry and slide inexorably into chaos. Zorg sees the woman he loves slowly going insane.

Sitting in the sun on the sand I felt like packing it all in. For three days I rode by myself whilst my crew held the journey together. I made for the nearest canal and talked to strangers on boats. As with every good traveller I told my life story in precisely five minutes knowing it wouldn't be a burden and they'd never see me again. I didn't do crying very well, but this time I cried deeply from my soul. I remember feeling I was a small dark shadow falling down a very deep hole, down and down, swirling unable to stop. I remember thinking that if I let this shadow fall too far, I would follow him too. For three days I felt like this, quietly trying to dissipate my sadness, but the masthead of incomprehensibleness would be raised for the rest of the year.

When I got back from the Europe ride, she was very pissed off, I think a little afraid at what she'd started. She'd checked into a hostel for the homeless in Upper Corris, near where we lived and when I found, out I drove round. It was a double fronted building not far from the slate quarries of Aberlefenni. The net curtains were dirty and it was unkempt, but the corridor in the side of the house where I met her was clean. My babies were shouting and laughing. She said that they were all right, and she was a good mummy and they were our little travellers. Willow had been on the Top of the World Expedition with us when he was three whilst she was pregnant with Juno. Willow had also been to Tobago and Sri Lanka; they'd all been on the Sahara part of the 2002 World Challenge and we'd all lived on a boat. I didn't know why she'd cracked up but she had.

Moto Challenge of Great Britain, July 2004

The Moto Challenge of Great Britain started at Santa Pod Raceway with riders experiencing quarter mile standing start times. Where else can a rider go from nothing to around 140 mph in about nine seconds – legally? There was something addictive about reaching such a speed so quickly that you had to keep on doing it. Some of the riders found enough time to do it 20 times, ruin a set of tyres and enjoy a riding experience they'd never known. Cracking one's motorcycling virginity is what this Challenge was all about. After a BBQ and an overnight stay, they rode via Avebury to mid-Wales where a hill climb was next on the agenda at Pontrydifendigaid near Tregaron.

Straightaway, the stories started to come out. You might say that the stories were 'outed'. Bikers were never straight, conservative about their bikes but otherwise broad minded. The tents were erected, the meal prepared by the catering crew, Justin and Eva and everyone was in a convivial mood, when one of my crew, Dave, just got into talking. He was the strong quiet type and although I hadn't known him for long, I knew that when he has something to say, you knew he'd been thinking about it for a while. "My brother thinks he's a lesbian."

"What?" I said. Everyone else's eye's just widened.

"Yea, he ought to come out but it doesn't really happen like that does it?" He paused and then continued, "he tried to cut his dick off as well, you know, he just didn't want to be a man. I had to take him to hospital, he was covered in blood." Robin was all ears, not sure if he could believe what he was hearing. We all were. This was a story *par excellence*. "This is a tale not even Hollywood could think up," Dave said, and after a pause, he said that there was more. "After he came out of hospital he ran off with a prostitute and they lived together. She said she was going to teach him how to be a man, and I think she did that alright. They lived together and for a while he didn't want to be a lesbian, he wasn't gay but simply cross dressed and all was well until the pimp turned up." We were stunned into silence. Without saying a word, we wanted to know everything. Dave was beginning to play to his audience and he did it very well. "So, they went on the run until the pimp caught them up, and he produced a gun and shot my brother in the leg and once again he ended up in hospital." Dave paused thoughtfully, as if wondering why he was telling a group of strangers something so intimate. I think he was also monitoring our ability to handle what he was saying. He said something about being one of nine children of which most of them had died. "There was always something happening in the family, it was as if we all had a weird gene, and there was something definitely strange about him. As a child he was always trying on girls clothes but you put that down to dressing up games. I never imagined it would come to this." There was a wind and most of the riders had retired for the night. You could hear a head of corn fall to the ground. "And that's not all!" The corn had dropped. "When he came out of hospital he was convinced he was a Red Indian, I mean, *really*, a Red Indian with the full head dress, the long hair, the chanting, I mean the full Monty and all of this in the centre of Wigan. I used to look away, I was mortified," he said smiling and then shaking his head as if in mock belief. "And that's not all! My other brother who loves line dancing dresses up as a Cowboy, the boots, the hat, the salopettes, everything, so we have an Indian and a Cowboy in the family, it's really weird."

I loved Dave's story. It was to do with a man and his brother, the strangeness of his family and almost a need to share it with people he didn't really know. Travellers told me the most intimate of secrets knowing full well that they would never see me again. Secrets are so powerful, so burdensome in that they take up so much space in your head, that they have to be off-loaded to make room for more.

The next day, the riders rode over to the Three Sisters Race Track, a charming little venue near Wigan, via the Bwylch y Groes, the highest mountain pass in Wales. We half expected Dave's brother to be dancing a rain dance by the Pier, a great photo opportunity, but no such luck. By the time this track event had finished, the riders and crew travelled to Cumbria crossing two of the finest short single-track roads in Europe, the Wrynose and Hardknott Passes. I, on the other hand, had given myself the onerous task of picking up two promotional girls at Wigan North Western Railway Station.

Helena arrived first, dropped off by her mum soon followed by Deborah whom I'd spotted at the Manchester Bike Show in January. She was working for Auto Trader Magazine, wearing one piece lycra, handing out leaflets and selling some product or whatever in a carrier bag for a pound. She stood out from the other promotional girls by virtue of her bubbly personality. We didn't really speak for six months other than a few text messages she sent me and a couple of rambling voice mails on my answer machine, obviously reminding me of the job I'd promised her. By the time I'd loaded their bags into the van, the riders were well on their way to Boot in the Lake District and we were to catch them up. It was easy conversation because having a job that surrounded them with men meant that professionally they were instantly comfortable with me. We chatted about this and that, the clothes they'd brought, types of make-up, what they were expected to do. My view was that they were to be my first Moto Challenge Girls, not dissimilar to Pit Lane Girls in Formula 1 or Moto GP.

When someone like Deborah alights in your life it's like a Gad Fly standing on the surface of water. So free is her spirit, that five minutes after she's gone, you are no longer sure if she was ever there. I sort of knew that instantly. By Boot we were best friends, after the event I was sure we'd probably not meet again. By Oban, the next day, she was preparing to ride with one of the crew.

By the time I'd paid the bill at our usual hotel, Corran House and then sorted out the riders, I was, as usual, the last man to be ready. So the girls could talk knowledgably about motorcycling it was agreed they be given a ride, and today's journey was in my opinion one of the best short routes in the world. Robin had already briefed Helena for 20 minutes, telling her how she should react if distressed and quite how to sit and ride. My briefing to Deborah was along the lines of *'hold on like fuck and DO NOT complain'*. For seven hours she sat head and shoulders above me on the back of my R1 before finally relenting and asked me if she could rest her legs on my knees as we travelled along. Early on we sped towards Fort William on roads that allowed me to catch up the back markers. It drizzled during the morning but soon the sun came out and as we headed into the west coast countryside. The views were pleasant enough and the sun and scattered showers made for a variety of weather that was very agreeable. I hadn't taken a pillion with me very often, Hennie couldn't get away from the children and it seemed somehow not right to ride with another woman if she was unable to be there herself. After our last conversation, I decided that now was as good a time as any to try and feel separated. Why the hell not? She didn't want me anymore. I had served my purpose and was cast in the role of a Salmon having spawned, and was now destined to swim upstream to die. In time I would drift back into the sea and be flung about by the tide until I floated on the surface belly up. My skin would go all white, and icky stuff would ooze out of my mouth and nose. Pity that. The pain was awfully acute, and whilst it would take many months to continue to get over it (if I ever could), I decided that as long as there was someone with nice soft breasts to land on, it's a pain I could bare.

So by midday at Badachro, with me and Deborah lounging in the leather seats in the Badachro Inn's conservatory over looking the harbour, the process that would marshal any long-term emotional damage into the nearest bin was thrust upon me. "Nice bike," she said, after being quiet for most of the journey, "it feels really nice, do you know what I mean?" I wasn't exactly sure, and rather presumed she really did like the bike. Excuse me, but for seven months your wife says she doesn't want you and then a 26-year-old lingerie model says she does, what do you do? Well, as a Catholic I'd struggle, so not being one that eliminated the need for guilt. As an arch Lutheran / Protestant work ethic orientated socially aware capitalist, I reckoned that my good works had brought me the success God intended and this was my small reward. As a Manchester lad with a snotty nose you don't say no to *nowt*. As a man whose tongue was hanging down to his turn-ups, I suffered immediate paralysis of any part of my brain, which disagreed with the word *'yes'*. A final quick checklist took me over the ethics barrier: I am not a monk; member of the Plymouth Brethren; I do like sleeping with girls and especially like woman in nice underwear. Bingo.

To state the obvious, I had begun to realise how pleasant it was to ride a sports bike with a pretty girl on the back, especially when there was nothing on the bike for her to hold on to. This was a relatively new experience for me. Let's not beat around the bush, if one can be excused the pun, but fast acceleration and hard braking threw her crotch into the base of my spine. When I shoved her back with my body, almost violently, to quickly reposition her to a point on the bike where some equilibrium could be urgently gained, I could take corners with more balance. This of course allowed my pillion to ride with me as one, safely and *harmoaniously*. "The vibrations of the bike are very nice," she said, "that's what I especially like."

"Oh, really," I said, nervously, but she captured the essence perfectly and I was rapidly catching on. "What sort of vibrations," I asked, "because the R1 is a very tight machine and I wasn't aware of any obvious mechanical movement."

"Well there is from where I'm sitting," she said, adjusting her trousers. Somewhere a little south of Durness and Scourie I looked round at Debbie and she looked at me and then she shifted to my side. I was doing 80 and slowed down to 70 when she cradled herself around me and lifted her left leg over the petrol tank as my clutch arm steadied her around her back. To compensate for her weight the bike leaned naturally to one side until she deftly swung herself round and hopped onto the tank to quickly swivel herself onto the seat to face me. There wasn't traffic but I didn't care if there was as she straddled her legs around my waist and leant back on the tank. As I stood up it allowed her more space to rest her head on the bars and as we were still doing 70 I lay on top of her and we pretended to fuck. We stayed like this for maybe 10 minutes and the best bit she said was looking up at the clouds as she lay down on the bike. She said she'd never seen the sky move from that position and when I stopped by a lay-by, we slowly untangled, climbed a small bank, quickly undressed and made love

As we rode along the top road the smile on my face reached the back of my head and as we arrived late for Robin's speech at John O'Groats I felt that today's ride was one of the best I'd had in my life. For three brief days Debbie and I were an item. I begun to realise that if this was the way my life was going to be, I'd rather have brief moments like this than a lifetime of pretence with someone who had decided they didn't love me.

The following morning, after the previous nights track session at Knockhill, I cleared the campsite and Debbie and I were the last to leave, so we popped into the shower and did it again. Harmony and bliss; a string quartet was playing outside and a waiter brought in a bottle of 1947 Dom Perignon nicely chilled. When we did it once again in the van later that night, I had security order Beluga Malossol Caviar from the Caspian, whilst Don Humungus de Toledo serenaded us with his 12-string guitar.

*

That night, after the event had been concluded successfully, I stayed with my dear friend Roger Murray on his boat in Bollington. Roger is one of the great men of the world. At 70, he biked across the US on my first Journey to the Top of the World in 1999. Three years later he rode across India during my 2002 Moto World Challenge and in 2004 he drove the back-up vehicle with Ted on the Moroccan tour. He also once employed 300 people for the northern office of McCann Eriksson, one of the big advertising agencies of the '80's and '90's. He was a tough man and turned the company around from having a 3 million portfolio of clients to that of 30 million, and was regarded as one of the best Chairmen in the business. Most of my ideas were mine, but always fashioned by him. There isn't a day that passes when we don't have a conversation and much of my business attitude was linked to his advice. It was difficult to know which part of him I related to most, brother, father or simply best friend, but having been divorced three times he patted me on the back and said well done.

*

The next day I shot off to Peterborough. I had a meeting with a sponsor and had to be there for eleven. Down to Uttoxeter and then east on the A50 past Derby until Melton Mowbray. The ride to Stamford via Oakham was exhilarating, more so on the way back when someone on a GSX 1000 caught me dawdling until I wound it up. He was still there and then he squirted past me when it was my turn to tail him. I had the GB event in my legs and after a training event like that, no one gets away for long, and when he found I was still stuck to his back wheel he sat up and waved me through. He rode like he knew the road and we exchanged nods and continued at a more civilized pace. The sponsor's meeting was good and it was agreed that they would use me in their campaign for next year. Clearly the GB event was going to grow and the sponsor wanted a much bigger presence.

When I got back to Roger's place, I put the bike in the van and drove back to my home near Machynlleth. After checking a few things in the office I danced alone in the living room for a couple of hours. For the first time in months I was really happy. Something had clicked into place. Emails sent to me immediately after the GB Challenge told of riders describing how their riding skills had dramatically improved and how much the challenge had improved their concept of bike riding. I don't think that it was an understatement when I said to my crew that we were actually saving lives.

Machynlleth, July 2004

That night, a couple of old friends, Tim and Bobby, drove up to the house whilst my Polish builder friend, Lechek, and me shared a drink. I hadn't seen Tim since my wedding when he served mushroom tea to my guests and caused chaos when no one could find their way to their accommodations. Whilst I was bouncing off the walls, jumping around to loud music, he immediately set about making dinner, and Lech just sat there, smiling and rolling up his Polish cigarettes. A low level optimistic outlook was part of the social-psycho environment indoctrinated by the communists before Solidarity overthrew Jarulewski. This *'victim spirit'* was suffered by Lechek's generation, which meant he expected nothing from life other than to work hard yet always be in debt. A dark humour was the only portent of hope the system had allowed him and his mates.

Bobby, meanwhile, was playing with her daughter and for a minute my world was whole. Even though I hadn't eaten properly I felt spiritually as if at last I'd had a good meal. When Tim brought out the chicken and the steak it was more food than I needed,

We chatted about old times. Tim and I went back 15 years and we began to reminisce about the School for Explorers I'd set up in the Peak District in 1992. The School was intended to be a summer camp for people wanting to sample a number of activities; ballooning, micro-lighting, rock climbing, photography, mountain biking and dance. Tim was the campsite manager and held it all together, more than I was capable of doing. Eighty members of the *'Girl's Friendly Society'* were booked in on the first week, and in an oversight I was prone to then, I'd forgotten to tell them to bring their own sleeping bags. They must have assumed it was Butlins and that everything was provided and when they arrived with no bedding, the nightmare began. After a preliminary visit by some stout matronly patron, the girls duly arrived, prim as you like from some prep school. I might have messed up with the sleeping bags but the local policeman managed to find me 100 blankets but that wasn't the problem. On Wednesdays, there was an alternative market in Sheffield city centre and these girls, who I'd managed to get sponsored by that august body, the Britannia Building Society, didn't give a fig about country life. By the middle of the week they came back armed with bongs and hubbly bubbly's and were too stoned to stand let alone go rock climbing, and by the weekend, once they'd shagged all my staff, were picked up by their headmistress who complimented me on having given them such a good time. The Britannia were not so pleased. Management hauled me into their office and asked me if I knew how close I'd been to a national incident? The News of the World love stories about drug fuelled hippie parties with under age girls, and if it weren't for the fact that I'd spent their money, obviously subsidising their drugs paraphernalia, they would have asked me for it back.

The second week we cared for 30 young people with special needs, none of whom would ever be able to write their name. They were a diverse lot and inhabited the strangest of shapes. Doris must have been in her forties and had a very small head. It was obvious that there wasn't a lot in it and she only ever repeated the one phrase she knew, "where the fuck am I?" she kept saying this over and over again for the whole week, and I just said that it didn't matter if she didn't know that, and after I gave her a couple of whiskies, she began to calm down. The Open Day was a disaster too. As usual I'd over promised, and the classic bike rally didn't happen at all, as neither did anything else. The brass band I'd hired played the same tune all afternoon. My girlfriend at the time, Millie, gave a master class in dance to an audience of 12 or 13 in a circus big top I'd bought with seating for 300 people of which I eventually sold it to someone who lost it in Africa. I'd erected it without permission from the Health and Safety Department on prime good-looking land knowing they would refuse. When, after the first week, they predictably served notice on me to close the camp down, they gave me the mandatory six weeks to comply. As the camp was only planned to be open for six weeks, the enforced closure was not really an issue. People from villages in the area came along out of curiosity. They'd all been reading in the papers that week about Glastonbury hippies drinking cans of Special Brew, and being quoted as saying they were better off on the dole than bothering to work for a living. In hard working areas around north Sheffield, that irritated the locals a lot and somehow we got lumped into the same mindset, which, was completely wrong. My crew was very hard working and we all had a commitment to do something different and unique. Ahead of our time, the collective heart was there, but the organisational skills and attention to detail was not. The brass band played on, and so did Millie. The disability carers got ripped in the caravan, and their charges, including Marcus and his mates with severe learning difficulties just wondered around in a haze.

On three acres of a dramatic piece of land on the Yorkshire side of the Peak District, I had established a campsite capable of housing up to 60 people. The most delightful element was the camp restaurant which had tables and chairs gaily lit by strips of coloured lighting. I'd insisted that the crockery was pot and not paper, but typically, had not stipulated when we should eat, so by ten at night, the soup was just beginning to be served. Problem was, people with special needs have to take their medication with their meal, and as this didn't happen until I managed to sober up the chef, they were going completely odd. Several had wondered off and weren't found until the morning, three had to be rescued from a 100ft rock fact at midnight and I caught two others with a blowlamp trying to inflate my hot air balloon.

Millie Manchester, 1992

Along with Suzanne, Linda and my present wife, Millie was one of the great loves of my life. She was beautiful with wide full lips and a face that could corrupt a man from a hundred paces. She had soft eyes, which she used to make up like Cleopatra. Roger introduced us to each other in her fathers

'Orangery', and although I was going out with someone at the time, fell in love with her instantly. She was trying to get out of a relationship with a guy from the old Yugoslavia, so it was several months before I asked her out. She was the lead performer in a contemporary dance company called 'Gestures'. The first time I'd ever seen contemporary dance was when I watched her perform at the Green Room in Manchester, and she was as beautiful as a peacock and as graceful as a swan. Because some old Honda 250 had just packed up on me, I needed a bike, so managed to persuade Raja, the then UK distributor of Indian Enfields, to give me the new 500cc version. All I had to do to claim my free gift was to ride it around the world. Immediately I did this I met Millie. When I think back, the choice I had to make was on a lower grading than life threatening, but it was still life changing. Every moment changes your life, but this is, for most people, one of the biggest, most talked about, most misunderstood apparitions of human behaviour; to let a beautiful young woman slip through your life and get snared by someone else you wouldn't even spit on.

After her show we snogged by the bike, and after I'd put my hand up her jumper, she invited me home. I followed her car on my lovely new bike, which because Eddie son Anthony, of Eddies 2 Wheels in Sale had put on a nice short exhaust, it thumped like a good 'un. During that ride I thought about the early years of my bike riding, which were not dominated by the culture except that it was my main means of transport. I bought my first bike when I was 16 in the days of Showaddywaddy and flared trousers. Then, you could ride anything up to 250cc on a provisional driving licence, and, unbelievably a 1000cc machine if you had a sidecar attached. I had a Honda 90 step-thru. I rode this everywhere, mostly on account of it's fuel economy, which gave me 90 miles to the gallon, unless I was carrying a bicycle on the back, as well as a TV, and clothes for another term at college. If I could rope it on, I did, and never for a moment considered getting pulled by the police. It never happened because, whilst it must have been unnerving to see a step-thru seriously laden down with all manner of goods, cracking on at such a fair pace, I was still going relatively slowly.

It would take an hour to cover the 40 miles between Glossop and Leeds, where I studied for a while and that included the famous Holme Moss mountain pass that dropped into Holmfirth but reduced me to walking speed on the way up. When I got my Enfield in 1992 I added to my assorted cargo, a small Border Collie dog called Charlie. She travelled in an orange box on a back rack specially made to carry five-gallon jerry cans for my impending first round the world ride. We travelled up the M1 from London to Manchester more times than I care to remember. In those days, even though I'd been doing journeys and getting mainstream sponsors for ten years, I was also happy taking time out. I knew that biking had a lot to offer me and I wanted to get involved in the sport with the same level of respect I approached some of my other projects. The only other bike I owned was a 1976 blue GS 750, which I was going to use in France in 1990. I'd started working in Newcastle upon Tyne with York Films, a small television production company who hired me to raise finance from broadcasting bodies in France and Japan, as well as set up interviews and story lines anywhere in the world about cycling. There was a six figure budget, a commission from BBC 2 and the Canadian Broadcasting Corporation, so it had to be good and I had to get around on time. Even though the bike I'd bought was a big leap from the step-thru, everyone else thought it a shocker and made me throw it away. It broke down three times in the first week and when I had it recovered to Mr Burnspeed in Newcastle, for the third time on the back of an RAC recovery truck, he recognised that this was bad for business, gave me some of my money back and told me to fuck off.

Millie's stepfather was reasonably wealthy but we shared a mutual dislike of each other. She lived in a council house with her three-year-old daughter who was called Zoe. She'd been dancing in Hong Kong and then Lubyiana, and only had the baby because her then boyfriend threatened to kill himself if she left him. Serbs are so serious and carry the weight of the world on their shoulders. So, having not laughed for five years she left him, and that night, once I'd parked my bike, ended up with me. I was unwholesomely in love with her, and would have had her dinner waiting on the table every night if that had been her wish. For a whole year I thought we were going to be together forever. All I said, was that I was going around the world on my bike, that I'd see her when I got back, and like a fool, believed her, when she said she'd wait!

Lechek Wales, July 2004

"I tell you a funny story, " Lech said suddenly, bringing me back to my living room in Wales. "I was in Warsaw, I was 16 years old and I was sniffing glue. You know I was addicted to it for two months, everyone was, and then one day I went for a walk in the forest when I saw a man hanging from a tree. When I looked at this man I saw he was wearing clothes exactly like mine and when I looked even closer I saw that he looked exactly like me. And when I looked at his face I saw that it was me." I didn't imagine Leck on glue, Prozac maybe, but glue seemed out of character. "But everyone was on it," he said, "during communism no one had any money and no one could afford any decent drugs. It was the drug of choice for a poor country and after that I never took it again."

Lechek was a mate who was doing some building work on a house I'd bought in the forestry nearby. He didn't express himself in a loud way and only needed a little quiet time to let his stories air. He was definitely not of the world an everyday

Polish person inhabits, and I guess that was why he was here. Like dust settling in a storm, people gravitate to their natural place in life.

Hunshelf Hall, 1989 - 1992

Tim was very quiet. His stories were deeply buried and only rarely surfaced. For several years he organised parties all over the world for very rich people. In between this, he rode a Laverda, went out with Big Sue, worked with me on the summer camp and was instrumental in my formative bike riding career getting off the ground. When I met him he was riding some made-up bike attached to a platform side car on which he'd bolted a duck he'd nicked from a kid's playground. The fact that you only needed somewhere to put your feet and something on which to hold on to made it perfectly legal. At that time, I'd ended up living in a farm called Hunshelf Hall, owned by Bruce and Angela. Located 1000 ft up on an escarpment a few miles north of Sheffield, the farm serviced 120 cows, nearly a valley's worth of tatty fields and oil seed rape and a river of cow slurry moving slowly through the yard. Within months of my arriving, Big Sue turned up, followed by wiry Tim with his round specs and little goatee beard. His bike riding was stymied by having to constantly take out the engine and reassemble it in the kitchen sink. His hands were perpetually oily and he addressed everyone by 'mate'. "Alright mate, yeah, no problem mate, should be easy to sort mate, yeah, it'll be alright mate." He was definitely one of those people that however hard he was finding life, he would never admit to it, and reckoned that everything always sorts itself out it you let it.

I first met Bruce after I'd been ballooning around the area and landed in a field near his farm, when he ran across the field and said hello. Bruce and I chatted for weeks across the Pennines. I was still living in Glossop at the bottom of the beautiful Snake Pass, still living with Linda, before Jainie and Millie. Linda and I were sort of together and we left Derbyshire to go and live near Bruce. She was a fine art screen printer, looked fantastic in a short skirt, and lived half the time in London. She was always blowing me out and the last time was over me not wanting food out of a can for my tea, and that was enough to sell the house and go our separate ways. I also used to keep my hot balloon in the kitchen and that pissed her off no end. I never really saw her again, and as usual I was a mess for months until some other woman relieved me of my desperate angst. A good shag keeps the doctor away, but as they say, a bad one is even better, so when I got the boot once again, I lived in my old 1967 open topped land rover for a few months, until Bruce rescued me, and said I could live at the farm in exchange for a free flight once every month. Thing was, he always wanted the same flight, down the valley behind his house so he could spy on whether one of his farmer friends wives was in a state of undress. He effectively gave me rent-free accommodation because my hot balloon was the only way he could see if, either before breakfast or early evening, whether she had her top off.

Capileira, August 2004

The alarm woke me at five the next morning and I felt shit. The taxi was already waiting, so I showered, grabbed my bags and headed for my train. Three hours later I was in a hired car driving along the Via Mediterranean from Malaga. I was heading towards the little mountain village of Capileira, where my young family were spending their summer holidays. It also meant another fruitless reunion with Henrietta. A little later, I was sitting with my two-year-old daughter by the fountain near my house, the moon was like a tusk suspended in the black sky. An old man brought a couple of mules to drink beside us, something he did every night. Whether it was his gesture to tradition, or part of the necessary means of transport to carry foodstuffs and farming implements to the barrancas, I didn't know, but the sound of the hooves against the cobbles was reminiscent of something timeless. Las Alpujarras is a pearl within a pearl; so beautiful and at one did I feel, living there. As Tatyana stood by the mules, chatting to herself, knowing she was next to her daddy, I felt happy that she was experiencing the cool breeze around her naked body and the animal smell of hot horsehair. The scent of bougainvillea mingled with the eucalyptus, whilst the small moon had descended to sit in the branches of a tree. A bright white sodium light also illuminated the tiny square. Tatty wondered off and I sat there alone with my thoughts, which were as incongruous as thoughts can get. That I ride one of the most sophisticated pieces of transport collectively invented by a myriad of geniuses, and just by me, and my little girl, an older form of transport snorted his breath to mist in the cool night air.

That evening, Hennie and I sat quietly on the terrace over looking the Poquiera Gorge. She sat silently as I talked about how it had all gone wrong. How two people can start out pulling together only to end up tearing it all apart. We were being gentle. It was still a mystery to me why she walked out and without apportioning blame, I told her how much I admired people who somehow managed to work through the hard times, which are part of any relationship worth saving. We had given each other three beautiful children, houses and money, and had been as close as anyone could be until that point when the axe fell on our little spirit. I said to her that I too had now reached that point when I couldn't carry on like this, and without looking, I heard her gently weep.

The following morning we were easier with each other. I was sleeping downstairs, and when I climbed up the spiral staircase and knocked on the hatch, she let me in. For a while I lay alongside her and we talked about the children. Two unusual people had come together and we were beginning to blame each other less. We were starting to address the consequences of those actions. I put my arms around her and once again she cried. "Do you know Nicky what your madness is?" she said softly, "because it isn't what your bikers think it is." I waited for her to tell me but the boys were beginning to make a noise. Her tear-lined cheeks pained me because I suddenly began to realise, that after seven months for her to still feel as she did, I must be the cause of some if not much of her distress. I knew that she was going to spend a week in a monastic retreat. I waited for to speak, but she didn't. She got up silently, dressed and left.

Most mornings whilst I lived in Capileira I took coffee in El Tilo's by the square near the top of the village. The owner was a biker and other than knowing I also rode a bike, he knew nothing about me. The warm understanding bikers have for each other was all we needed. My children sat on the bar stools and watched sport on the TV whilst I grabbed a few minutes to write and assess how the rest of the year was shaping up. I was also trying to put together the new life that was being forced on me so sent a text message to Millie asking if she minded me being in touch. She said call back in five so I did. We had communicated during my trip to Morocco and again during my Moto Challenge of Europe, but as my head became increasingly more stable, she responded more, less fearful of how my own signals of dysfunction brought to mind her own. Millie and I would have still been together had it not been for her complete inability to cope with my absences abroad, probably the one major fault Hennie and I had allowed to unscrew our own relationship. All of my journeys have strived to deal with the need to be away compared with the need to maintain a home life, and I have to admit that I have failed.

For Millie, my Enfield journey was our nemesis. All was well when she met me in Alexandria; by Delhi she pleaded with me to come home. Come Calcutta I heard her in bed with another man, and conversations that followed in Bangkok, Perth and along the Stuart Highway left me in no doubt that I'd blown it once again. In contrast, Hennie held out substantially longer. She managed eight years of my severe adventuring and madness including several major group expeditions and three motorcycle navigations of the world before she completely cracked, so by comparison I guess she did rather well.

I ordered another coffee. The boys were watching the Moto GP of Germany and unusually Valentino Rossi was laying in an uncharacteristic forth place before whacking his underpowered Yamaha M1 to a victory podium finish. The new engine Yamaha had promised him was to be installed probably for the next event and it was expected that this would tip the balance in his favour (as if he needed any extra help). Sete Gibernau was the great Spanish hope and one of these three great heroes' would be crowned the finest rider of his generation this year. I looked at my little lads, glued to every twist and turn, and wondered how they would interpret the motor biking content I had introduced to them in their young lives. The dangerous downside was more than compensated by the incredible companionship and brotherhood the sport gave anyone who took their riding seriously. The geographical freedom it also gave was a simple and beautiful gift. When I set off to bicycle around the world in 1981, it was with the sole purpose of giving myself a real education. I also wanted to get away from my home life. My working class upbringing, whilst solid, was limiting and the council estate I was brought up on was inevitably myopic. Whilst I had easily created a mental distance, it was the physical distance I needed to work on, and bicycling long miles every weekend showed me a wider world. I knew early on that nothing of worth need ever be undervalued, that money was only one example of a value you placed upon yourself, but that there were others which money could not buy. So I stood somewhere between wanting money, and not actually needing it, but the hugely usable energy needed to break through this financial glass ceiling and class inertia, was, if harnessed, the greatest talent I had.

After a long siesta followed by more play and pizza, I took my small brood back to the house. It was now dark outside and a storm had come and gone. The lightening had brought with it the thunder, and the breeze had sweetened the air. Willow and Tatty had briefly danced in the rain, but were now firmly tucked up in their beds. It was midnight and I had a few moments to myself to reflect on this mid waypoint in my year.

My domestic calendar was now over, and preparations for my international events were well under way. Flight arrangements for the Alaska, North American and round the world journeys were booked, sea freight containers to New York secured, air freighting space organised, US motoring insurances finalised, hotels across Canada as far as Dawson Creek paid for and my back up crew were just about in place. A key figure in my plans was my best long-term friend Elspeth Beard. It was unthinkable that she should not travel with me. Without her, my professional life would be made immeasurably more difficult. We met in 1992, when, after I'd finished my around the world Enfield ride, we journeyed to one of Bernt Tesch's world travellers meetings held each year near Aachan. Bernt had put us in contact with each other, so we drove in her car to his venue where we were both to give a talk. As both of us were impecunious in the extreme, and Bernt didn't pay any expenses, she slept in the back seat and I slept outside. We were never an item and looking back, that was a good thing. We had something much stronger, a life long friendship, something I had rarely achieved with any of my girlfriends.

Over twenty years ago Elspeth spent two years motorcycling around the world and became only the third woman ever to do so. The male orientated motorbike press who universally refused to acknowledge her achievement had shabbily treated her. Journeying solo around the world was more than just riding a motorbike, which whilst being a tremendous undertaking, it required more. Journeying alone around the world necessitated a total commitment to being away from home, and away from family and friends. It also took you away from every conceivable point of reference you had ever learnt. If you also recognised the metaphysical content of such a journey, then you laid down your soul to fate. As well as her motorcycling, she flew her young son Tom around Australia in a hired Cessna. Being a resourceful and quite famous architect, she single-handedly renovated a mighty 150ft tall Victorian water tower in the heart of Surrey. Occasionally we had dinner on the flat roof overlooking half the county, and it was easy to see how one could detach oneself from the rest of the world. She said she needed that ability to shut herself away, and whilst for some it would have been a prison, it was for her, an escape. It was a long while later that she admitted to having had moments, in her very strong life, when she wanted to throw herself off the top.

*

By the early hours of the morning, the cicadas in Capileira had at last become quiet. I was still on the phone, calling Seattle to book rooms in Whitehorse on the Alaska Highway. I called my old friend Charles in Dawson Creek, and then Gary at the Sealaska Inn in Hyder, and just booked up the whole hotel. Up the creek the bears would still be catching salmon with their paws. When I took my 22 riders around the world in 2002, an acquaintance, Ron Ayres introduced us to Hyder as one of the great biking destinations in North America, and in the bar late at night everyone got completely drunk.

The next day, after a week of being away, Hennie returned from her Monastic retreat and true to form, she was now a converted Buddhist. Bless her. For a while she gave me cards that wished me 'peace and love' and when I told Roger, he chuckled. Who wouldn't? I was about to go through a divorce but I still loved the girl. She was a braveheart. I regarded that as one of the highest compliments I knew how to give, and still felt her very close to my own heart. But who was this girl? It had taken nearly nine years to get to this question. Obviously nine years too late, but there must have been a lot to know I never knew about. The next night she invited herself to dinner, so I got in a pizza and some wine and we got merry and enjoyed each other's company immensely. She was looking really good, and said she was so incredibly chuffed about her life. I sunk into the ground a bit, but recovered and gave her a watery smile. Right! Don't beautiful people just sometimes get on your tits? But then, over worked wannabe oligarch that I am, I began at last to realise that no one has a right to stand in the way of someone's personal happiness; and some other man's joy even though I felt he ought to be eviscerated. I would have liked to hang, draw and quarter any man who went near her and feed his innards to the crows, but of course my solicitor said I mustn't do that. When I told Marilyn, who is representing me, that I thought my wife needed a fairly firm spanking, she shot bolt upright in her office back in Machynlleth and said I could only do that *after* we were legally separated.

She'd done her bit, gave me kids, looked after them, blew a fuse, needed to get on with what she wanted to do instead of being engulfed by my nonsense. After looking after three children under six and a half solidly for a whole week, my head was turning into worm meat, so I guess I began to understand, and from then on, we were friends.

True love they say runs a funny winding course. My present marital dilemma started back two years ago when the Global Rider journey took me overseas for four months in 2002. After a month at home this was followed by the Motorcycle World Challenge journey, which kept us apart for another three. Add to this, lots of meetings in the UK that took me away for the night and I was absent from my family home for 10 months out of 12. I thought we could handle it. Professionally it was a success, but personally it laid down the foundations for Hennie's uncertainty. I was an adventurer, what could I do? Not be an adventurer like she cannot be a mother? For me it started the night when my round the world riders made it to Hua Hin.

Thailand, October 2002

It must have been Day 48 out of the 96 days we'd planned to complete the journey and as an overnight it was only a morning's ride south of Bangkok. My friend Simon, who lived there had organised a party in a local bar in a quieter part of town and after all we had done, we all needed a drink. Bangkok represents other challenges if you've never been there before, and the riders were tired. I knew that if we entered one of the most entertaining cities in the world they'd go out and be entertained and I wanted them to be prepared. Get used to alcohol for a start. We'd been living extremely straight lives, almost like athletes, certainly we had been really dedicated to motorcycling around the world in less than three months, and I suppose this was a good halfway point and a good time to let our hair down. The bar was off a back street and the riders kept buying me shots of Thai whisky. Somehow I started talking to the pretty bar manager and by the end of the evening I was so drunk she had to walk me to my hotel. As ever, the alcohol continued to percolate into my bloodstream so by the time we entered the lobby, I was unaware of her keenness, which I would liked to have witnessed, but unfortunately couldn't stand let alone see. The porter must have carried my legs because she was medium to petite, and even though nature is endlessly resourceful when it wants to perpetuate the species, a small Thai woman cannot usually carry a fully-grown man. On the other hand, this woman was going to rape me and I think she would have dragged me across a jungle clearing should it have been necessary, and no one cared to stop her. It was as if I was catatonic. I wanted to speak but couldn't. This was definitely different. I was so pissed I couldn't fart let alone fuck, and the more she kept jumping on me, the less conscious I became. Somehow I managed to push her away. It wasn't like before when I was a single man. I was married now and for the first time in my life I had begun to learn to resist the cheap sensations of casual sex in a dangerous place. The love I had for my wife and family somehow saved me from a pattern of behaviour, from which for years, I'd longed to escape.

Thailand was, aside from the diesel fumes and scruffy roadside, a particular kind of paradise. The temptations were dreadful which made you feel Saintly if you resisted and Godly if you succumbed. It was a win win situation because as superficial as it might sound, beautiful women laughed at your crap jokes and thought everything you said earnestly had great meaning. Everyone it seemed was a Buddhist in Bangkok. *"I'll have a Margarita with ice, my son….*ah, that reminds me of the last time when I had six in Palm Springs and then slept in a ditch."

The next day, Matt found me in a heap on the floor in my room. As an experience, it wasn't even very existential, just stupid. I said goodbye, the girl grabbed at me to stay but Matt pulled me free, got me ready and put me on my bike. A few hours later we all rolled into town. We were soon on Khaosan Road, *the* party street in this part of Bangkok. Not difficult to find and not hard to make friends in a hurry as we had only one day to rest before heading up north to an area around the River Mekong. On the previous ride, I met a new friend, Daniel Vetter, from a few notes I left on the Internet. He was Mr Motorcycle Fixit around these parts and also specialised in knowing Cambodia. I needed any kind of help and very kindly he was there for me.

Members of something sounding like the Bangkok Bikers Club set up a long table right out on the main road. The owner of our hotel was a biker and one of the wealthiest men in Thailand. His immaculate convertible white Rolls Royce, one of 20 such vehicles he owned, would be parked outside and *no one* would touch it. All the lads were sat at the table, quaffing beers and laughing, a nice girl within everyone's talking distance. Camera crews turned up and filmed us and some dignitary said a few words, which of course none of us understood. As I looked around, it was with a sense of real pride. What these riders had done was remarkable. It wasn't just their riding 15 000 miles across three continents in six weeks that was impressive, it was because they might never do it again and were making the most of every single day.

"For God's sake Elspeth," I said, "don't let me drink anything, you know what I'm like." She vowed to watch me and did a crap job. I necked ten bottles of some blue stuff, jumped in a taxi with Jonathon, the bus driver, and ended up in a brothel. "That was quick," I said to Jonathon, "how the fuck did we get here? Was it your idea or mine?" Before he had time to answer he was whisked away by a wizened and frail old lady who handed him to a girl. I was then taken to a room to choose from perhaps 30 girls sitting on chairs in a circle. So far so good, but as I chose my date for an hour, the blue stuff I'd knocked back was beginning to take effect. 'Oh, not another ridiculous encounter,' I said to myself before slowly beginning to remember less. I do recall being washed absolutely all over, tenderly and very thoroughly, and then, somehow, I came to my senses once again. It was all right getting fucked 12 years ago on my Enfield journey, but not any more. I had three small children to think about and to this girl's surprise I asked to leave.

Jonathon carried me to the taxi and took me back to my room on Khaosan. The next day, everyone except me, would journey to the bridge over the River Kwai, and over the next few days, to

Nong Khai in the north. Elspeth would manage this part of the trip whilst I made calls from my hotel and finalised the next part of the journey. I called the Enfield factory where they were sponsoring the India leg and set up with their PR people a press campaign from Madras to Delhi. I didn't know then how successful that was going to be. It seemed to me, that whatever event happens to you in life, it is just as it should be, because there didn't seem anything I could do, to make it all change.

*

At Sheffield there was a sign on the platform that read: *Caution. Trains Passing Quickly Stand Back From The Edge.* To me that was how I felt I'd led my life. To others who knew me, it could have read; *Nice View Sit Here by Seat of Pants.* My farmer friend Bruce lived a little north of here and I loved living in his house. When I wasn't flying to pay my rent, I flew every other day and made money barnstorming around South Yorkshire, charging local farmers to fly across their land. I flew on a regular basis from North Sheffield to Doncaster or across the Pennines, and enjoyed my humble role as the aeronautical equivalent of farm pet.

Hot Air Ballooning Great Britain, 1990

Often I flew through the clouds, regularly up to 7000 ft, and then back down again to skim across fields of wheat and barley. For ten years I flew, amassing 3000 hours. There were many memorable flights, but one that stuck in my mind was when I took a farmer and his wife along with his friend the local butcher. The weather was good, we flew easily, and the balloon was stable, as was the envelope of air that carried us along. After a while we popped through the clouds and sat there, on those castles in the sky that from down below look as if they would support your weight. Above the clouds the sky was a deep summer blue, and hot. We sipped champagne as we drifted along and chatted amiably. I knew that they were in awe of what they saw. Who wouldn't be? Below the clouds, everything was grey and dull. Below cloud life had no sparkle. Above was a land of make believe where you could lean out of the basket and touch the pinnacles and towers that comprise this mythical landscape. As we descended through the white mist, it took a minute or so, the world went silent and the air became damp until we popped out from beneath the cloud base. A few minutes more and I'd descended another 6000 ft and was beginning to look for a suitable place to land, and when I saw a field without crop directly on our flight path I briefed my passengers to 'watch their line of approach, hold on to the rope handles of the basket, stow away all valuables and bend knees as we hit the ground'. Now the chap who arranged for me to fly this small party was called Fred, and he hadn't listened to me because he was too busy taking photographs of the shadow of the balloon, which was racing behind us. The ground rushed towards us as I engaged in a textbook landing except for the fact that the basket gently tipped over. We all ended up in a heap in the bottom of the basket, and Fred, who wasn't holding on, rolled out. Having lost his beefy 12 stone the balloon immediately gained inertia and took off again. His wife screamed, we all righted ourselves, and I told her that everything was fine and that this wasn't the first time I'd lost someone. I didn't mean it quite like that, but she screamed again and was nearly hysterical before she suddenly went very quiet. I said that we'd pick her husband up in the next available flat field and because she said nothing I assumed that she was now calm. We climbed steadily; 100ft – 200ft until we rounded out at 350ft when Fred's wife went white, clearly wanting to say something but somehow couldn't. "It's all right," I said, "this happens all the time. I've done a lot of flying," followed by the fateful words, "I do know what I'm doing, you know!"

Now, everyone knows also that as soon as you have to say this there is a chance that you're bluffing. That actually, you don't know what the hell's happening and by simply doing nothing you are really waiting for things to sort themselves out. There's a Yorkshire saying that *if in doubt, do nowt and say nowt,* when suddenly, out of the blue, Fred's wife said with a splutter,

"But he's still there."

"I know," I said, "he rolled onto the ground and we'll pick him up at the next field."

"No, he's still there" she said more assertively,

"What?"

"He's there,"

"Where?"

"There, under the fuckin' basket yer stupid man," and I looked over the edge of the basket and saw Fred hanging upside down.

"Fuck me," I shouted, "you're right, why the fuck didn't you say something earlier?" Fred had got his right foot loosely entangled in a bit of rope that I used to attach the balloon bag to the basket and he was hanging upside down. I nearly shat myself. If he stretched his ankle his foot would have slipped out of the rope and he would have cratered the oil seed rape field directly below. "For God's sake Fred," I shouted, "don't stretch your fucking leg and put your hands behind your head." We were 300ft above the ground, flying straight and level at 30 knots and I reckoned if he did fall, his arms would cushion his landing. I mean, this wasn't in the fucking textbook. I immediately yanked the ripcord to release some air and then compensated by burning some gas to gain more buoyancy. I literally panted with panic. My heart was pounding. Rip, burn, rip burn, I alternatively pulled open the ventilation panel at the crown of the envelope and turned on the tanks to wrest control of the balloon and descend in as smooth a manner as possible. At what seemed like an age, we slowly rounded out and begun to descend. First 100ft, then 50ft. Everyone was quiet. All was well except that because the ground wind had now picked up we rattled away across field after field unable to land, until I saw one big enough and without anymore mucking about came down for the final approach. "Hold on Fred," I shouted, "here we go," and we zoomed into a field full of cows which scattered to all corners when Fred's head, which I used as a brake, hit the deck until we eventually came to a complete standstill after dragging him for more than 200 yards. Thing was, with cows come cow pats and Fred hit about 2000 of the fucking things and when he walked over to greet me he was covered in shit from head to foot. He wiped his eye's and his mouth and made as if to speak.

"Tha' were fuckin' great," he said, "tha' were fuckin' best ride of ma life," shook my hand and gave me a tenner for a tip.

*

I was off to Malaga to pick up my kids and the plan was to cycle home with them before I met up with my riders in New York. It was a good opportunity to go and visit my in-laws as it would probably be the last time I'd see them as a married man. I liked both Beatrice and Richard, partly because they had been unstintingly nice to me but also because they were two of the funniest people I'd ever met. They were unaware of this singular talent because it was the depth of their seriousness that always made me laugh. Richard fast tracked from Eton to the City and was never afraid to broadcast his views about anything at any time; the war, the government, people on social welfare. He especially reveled in discussing the life of his eldest daughter. Henrietta's mother, Beatrice, sort of German war orphan au pair who married a rich toff, recently took up, and I'm sure for reasons only known to her, a unique and unambiguous position in positively supporting everything

Henrietta did. Whilst their main topic of conversation was contradicting each other, you'd need the psychological profile of Ghengis Khan to ask the question why. Moreover, Richard had suddenly discovered jokes and while I was well ensconced in the basic framework of the family, I was also soon no longer to be technically an in-law, so Richard said things to his daughter which he didn't always share with me; "did I tell you the one about the woman who fancied playing with her husband's sex toy only for him to ask her if she knew where he'd put his new tartan vacuum flask, *ha ha ha*?!" That sort of thing. Brother-in-law Charlie had escaped to Melbourne with a splendidly breasted woman called 'Bells', and sister-in-law Emma, who, as beautiful as Hennie, equally found men a complete mystery and was clueless about the use of said item once you'd been to bed with it.

That night, Aunty Em took me out for dinner, after which we went to see a friend of mine in the Coopers off the King's Road. Ant proceeded to tell us, without the slightest encouragement, how women have been overheard commenting on the size of his dick, at which point I put my head in my hands and asked myself which planet it was that I lived on and flew the next night to Malaga.

*

After arriving at the airport, I unpacked my bicycle and cycled to the edge of the city. After eating a fish tapas, I settled in a hostel nearer the centre before setting out the following morning for Las Alpujarras east of Granada. The Sierra Nevada Mountains stretched from Granada to Almeria and Las Alpujarras was a region that comprised of scattered settlements of white washed villages, hamlets which have retained their traditional Berber architecture - terraced clusters of grey-white box-shaped houses with flat clay roofs - which is still common in the Rif and Atlas

Mountains of Morocco. They all nestled on slopes where sometimes you could hear the haunting cry of the Hoopoe. It took me 14 hours to cycle to Orgiva and my eyeballs stuck out from my cheeks like a bullfrog on a stick. I crawled into bed and the next day crawled back onto my bike and rode 12 miles uphill to Capileira at 4500 ft. Hennie and me got on well for five minutes then argued. I looked after the kids for the day and then over breakfast we chatted better. Whatever happens we always seem to rebalance to a point where we actually like each other: correction; we remember that we've had three children together and realize that if we don't make an effort to work things out it'll be hell for the next 20 years; and then, I put Willow on an attached smaller tag-a-long bike and Juno in the pull-a-long pod. With a wave, we set off, and we don't know where.

The route to Trevelez was hard. There was hardly a flat stretch of road. I was pulling two boys, our entire road junk and a very long bike, maybe 70 kilos in all. We pushed more than we cycled but I reckoned it was good fitness training for when I attack my old round the world record. I'd already lost 14 pounds and felt quite good. I was fast enough and knew my way around. Point to point on my Yamaha was my *stock-in-trade*. It was simply what I do best.

By Trevelez it was 38 degrees so we grabbed some lunch. By early evening we checked out a pension in a bar in a small village and a woman with a greedy smile wanted 50 euros so I said to the lads that we should move on. We hit a long hill and for an hour we pushed our load to the top. Poor little lads having to learn Dad's little lessons of life. I'd rather climb a mountain and sleep under a bush than subjugate myself to greed. As I was explaining this idea to Willow, we reached the summit when I glanced a notice from the corner of my eye. I rode back and read about a *Casa Rural* 400 metres up a dirt track to our left. There was a telephone number, I called and yes there was space and it was inexpensive. We climbed up and found the most delightful white fronted house beside a freshly laid terraced courtyard over looking a valley settling down with all the magenta colours of a sunset. An elegant dining room was next to the kitchen and the bedroom was exquisite with a view down the valley that couldn't be bought in Manhattan, Paris or Rome. "Boys!" I said, "life is all about taking a chance on something maybe working out better;" and that night I dined on quail. The lads had stuffed chicken followed by a cream pudding. My *postre* was accompanied by a marmalade wine and for a precious and small moment it seemed to me that life couldn't get any better. I tucked my lads into bed, and kissed them goodnight, knowing how the cool valley wind would flow over their hot faces and make them sweeter for the morning. I chatted to Walter and Eric the Dutchmen then sat quietly outside. The sun had long since set and the sky had turned from the deepest of reds and blues to black.

There was music playing from the village of Berchules. They were celebrating New Years Eve in August because ten years ago the electricity failed on December 31st, so they decided to make use of a more regular summer supply and make it a cult event. My phone bleeped. Unexpectedly it was a text from Millie. She was sailing off the coast of Croatia and would be back in Manchester later in the week. This was a surprise and she inadvertently reminded me of a time in my life I revisit rarely. I knew I wouldn't be able to see her until after the 96 day journey in December, unless I squeezed in an hour or so before my flight to New York, but that was unlikely. I'd seen her twice in 10 years and before that we met in Alexandria, then Cairo. 12 years ago I biked around the world on my Enfield. It had broken down in Venice and again near Damascus and more terminally across the Nubian Desert. I hitched a ride with a truck from St Catherine's Monastery to near Talaat Herb Street by the Air France building and near the Golden Hotel where I stayed at the start of my journey to the source of the Nile. When we met at the airport I wouldn't take a cab and made her take a bus into the city. I remember the next day we took the train to Alexandria and holed up in a cheap room. We talked; she was upset because someone had stolen the scooter I'd given her for Christmas. She'd lent it to her ex and he'd left it out all night. She was a mess and in a way so was I. I wasn't unsympathetic but I just thought that if we got into bed and fucked all our bad stuff would go away, and it sort of worked out like that, but not quite. She was gorgeous and I adored her, but I still had to go around the world on my bike. Leaving Millie behind was the third hardest decision I have ever had to make.

Africa, 1983

The first hardest decision was in 1983, when I left my mum to die as I set off to cycle to the source of the White Nile. She was dying of cancer and the prognosis for her was to live anytime between two years or three months. She lived for three months. I was in Uganda and staying as a guest of Brother Elliot, a missionary Father of the Sacred Heart of Jesus in the outback near Gulu. There was a civil war raging all around and in complete ignorance I was cycling along the Bomba Road, reputedly then, one of the most dangerous roads in Africa. For a brief few days when Brother Elliot wasn't introducing me to friends or showing me his geography classroom covered in magazine pictures, I would sit in his living room drinking sweet hot coffee, tune into the World Service on the radio or flick through 'Time' magazine. Natassia Kinski was on the front cover. She was the daughter of mad eyed Klaus who starred in most of Werner Hertzog's films, notably with Claudia Cardinale in *Fitzcarraldo*. That film was about a rubber baron's desire to build an opera house in Manaus deep in the Amazon rain forest. When I saw the film for the first time it inspired me to retrace his route with a girl who oddly once wrote for Newsweek.

That year, I'd been on the road every day for thirteen months and sort of chanced on the Mission whereby Brother Elliot and his companion Father Joshia invited me to rest for a while. I hadn't seen tarmac since Juba in Sudan and there was still only red dirt roads to ride on, so I accepted his offer of hospitality. Every night we sang Benedictine and at seven fifteen, dinner was served. That night, a storm brewed. I remember saying goodnight and walked over to my cell to pack my bags ready for another day on the bike. The first few drops of rain fell; large bulbous splashes from dark billowing clouds. The wind rose and, like an ebb-tide, receded to blow stronger the next time. A flash of lightening appeared to detonate the crackle of thunder as a barrage of drum-fire grumbled in the air. I'd been asleep only to be awakened by the storm raging directly overhead. Continuous sheet lightening turned night into day and the roar on the corrugated tin roof was deafening. I wrote up what I saw in my diary:

Diary 13th June 1983 Gulu

Stroboscopic effect of flickering lights panning across the sky as if the intensity of the flash raised the tempo of the rain, the beat of the drum from the corrugated roof. The rain dribbled from the corrugations, motionless in the shivering light and a spider hangs grimly, swinging. It won't be long. This is a spider-demolishing storm. The flashes made the mosquito-netting look like the lines on a TV screen. A cathode ray tube view of an electric storm and in the distance an empty field, the only empty space where direction is free from foliage. In the near distance with the emptiness behind, a tree raised her two arms and a woman is hanging. How I beckon her to come to me, how I beckon her to umbrella her way through the rain to tell me it's not her hanging in the tree, arms outstretched for all to see yet all will not see because it's her and me, the mosquito net

2002, Global Rider TV series
R1 in the Sonora Desert in Northern Mexico

1982, Bicycled the length of Indonesia
Here resting outside Raffles Hotel with a mob of Miss Singapores!

Clockwise from top left

2002, Moto World Challenge
In India you see crashed trucks like this every 20 miles

1992, Round the World Enfield Journey
The bike was surprisingly good in the snow

1984, Coast of Britain journey
The finish in Blackpool

1984
Cycled 4802 miles around the coast of Britain in 22 days

1996, Pan American journey in Nicaragua
I did this in 30 days, but failed to beat the car record of 19 days so kind of dismissed it as a failure

1982
Crossing the Equator in Sumatra

Clockwise from above

1996, Costa Rica
On the Pan American Highway when I failed to beat the car record of 19 days
1992
Finish of the Enfield world journey at the manx GP, IOM - I did my own sign-writing!
1996
Pan American journey and where I punctured in Chile
1983
Source of the White Nile bicycle journey in Burundi

2002, Moto World Challenge
The whole group at the Enfield factory in Madras

2002, Moto World Challenge
On the road in India, Elspeth in the foreground

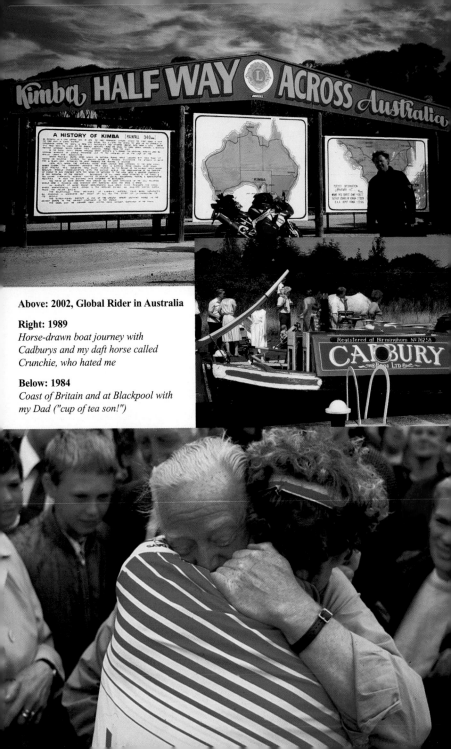

Above: 2002, Global Rider in Australia

Right: 1989
*Horse-drawn boat journey with
Cadburys and my daft horse called
Crunchie, who hated me*

Below: 1984
*Coast of Britain and at Blackpool with
my Dad ("cup of tea son!")*

Above: 1994, Black Country to Black Sea Expedition
Crossing the Channel - 16 hours from Ramsgate to Calais, I just followed the ferries

Right: 2002, Thailand
If you think I've got a mad job, what about this nutter; what's he doing, ploughing water?

Below: 1992, Enfield in the Dolomites

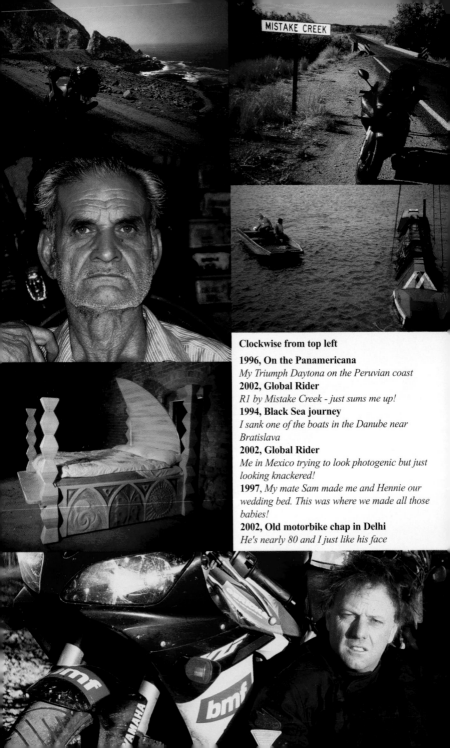

Clockwise from top left

1996, On the Panamericana
My Triumph Daytona on the Peruvian coast
2002, Global Rider
R1 by Mistake Creek - just sums me up!
1994, Black Sea journey
I sank one of the boats in the Danube near Bratislava
2002, Global Rider
Me in Mexico trying to look photogenic but just looking knackered!
1997, *My mate Sam made me and Hennie our wedding bed. This was where we made all those babies!*
2002, Old motorbike chap in Delhi
He's nearly 80 and I just like his face

Clockwise from top left

2002, Global Rider in Australia
I just love long trains
2002, Global Rider in Australia
The sign says it all
1994, *Black Sea boats in Romania near the enormous Iron Gates*
2002, Global World Challenge
Me in Thailand
2002, Global Rider in Southern Texas
I went flying with this guy and with my money he went to buy his groceries

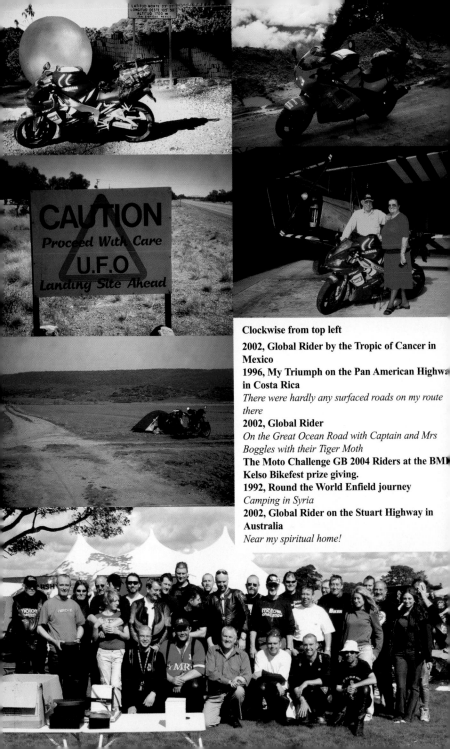

Clockwise from top left

2002, Global Rider by the Tropic of Cancer in Mexico

1996, My Triumph on the Pan American Highway in Costa Rica
There were hardly any surfaced roads on my route there

2002, Global Rider
On the Great Ocean Road with Captain and Mrs Boggles with their Tiger Moth

The Moto Challenge GB 2004 Riders at the BMF Kelso Bikefest prize giving.

1992, Round the World Enfield journey
Camping in Syria

2002, Global Rider on the Stuart Highway in Australia
Near my spiritual home!

Clockwise from top left

- Round the World 2003 Riders meet at Nick's Moto Challenge HQ April 2004
- Fellow Competitor Paul Uden was understandably overwhelmed to recognise his father was indeed one of the bronze statues.
- The 'Pass of Cattle' and Karl Holdsworth stops to admire the view with Helen the delightful model.
- Spean Bridge Commando Memorial and the 'burlesque' posing team of 'Norfolk and Chance', L – R Chris Kelly, Martin Fox and the eventual winner, Kiwi all rounder Matt Carter.
- The generous South African couple Bruce and Gail Bullock at peace on the scenic 'Pass of Cattle', later at John o'Groats he had to 'cough up' £500 to charity, matched by the Challenge Riders, for tipping glorious Gail off the bike "put me off that bike just once and you'll have to pay dearly for it!" thankfully it only hurt his wallet.

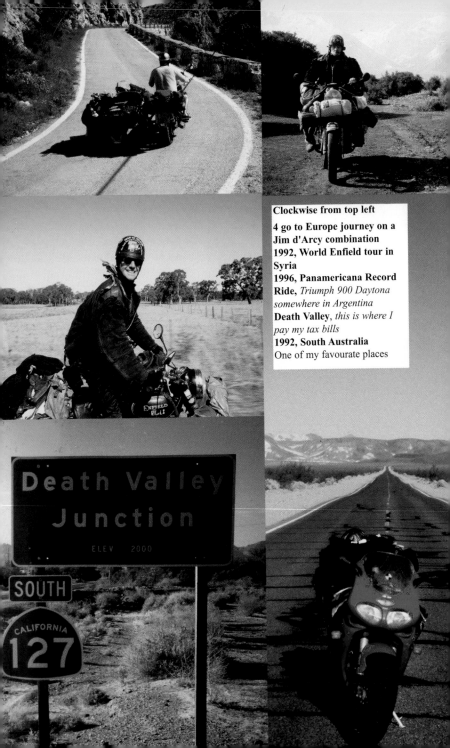

Clockwise from top left

4 go to Europe journey on a Jim d'Arcy combination
1992, World Enfield tour in Syria
1996, Panamericana Record Ride, *Triumph 900 Daytona somewhere in Argentina*
Death Valley, *this is where I pay my tax bills*
1992, South Australia
One of my favourate places

Clockwise from top left

Hanging around in Mexico
2002, Global Rider in Delhi
The Enfield boys at the Bullet Club of India
2002, Global Rider Australia
2002, Moto World Challenge Outskirts of Madras
2002, Global Rider Nong Khai Sculpture Park
2002, Moto World Challenge Uluru

Clockwise from top left

2002, Moto World Challenge
Outskirts of Madras
2002, Moto World Challenge
Me in Thailand
2002, Global Rider
Completely amazing man spent his life making these sculptures by hand
Sign in Thailand
2002, Moto World Challenge in India

ยินดีต้อนรับสู่เมืองคนงาม

WELCOME TO CITY OF NICE PEOPLE

2002, Global Rider By the Great Australian Bight
Across the Nullarbor Plain
Tin Man sculpture South Australia Hotel San Antonio
Not one of the hotels I stay in!
2002, Moto World Challange
People in India
2002, Moto World Challange Enfield journey in India

1997, London World Record Finish
Me and Hennie: I'm a sucker for a pretty girl. She's only got to smile at me and I go all stupid!

the great divide, iron bars separate a lifetime. But there's a hole in the netting, maybe there's a hope, now all I have to do is gnaw at the iron bars with my teeth.

Alone in a storm in Uganda was the only occasion I could bring myself to write about my mother who was dying. A feeling of the extraordinary condensed on my sweaty arms, legs and sweaty face as I looked out of that window. My mother had given me the most extraordinary experiences from which I'd forced myself to recover in order to survive. She was a consummate drunk who was desperately unhappy in a post war marriage. When she could drink no more she would be utterly oblivious of her urinating fully clothed in front of me. As a five year old, I naturally blamed it on the puppy. When I eventually returned to Cairo in late July, a letter awaited me telling of my mother's death. I was in Groppi's Cafe where I always had my breakfast when in town. When I read the date she died, I knew I'd experienced something I couldn't explain – it was June 13th, and I burst into tears. Tears of relief. Good woman though she was, entrapped in a worthless emotional relationship that gave her zero value, there was hardly a moment in my life when I felt she could communicate with me. There was hardly a moment during my childhood that she made me feel good about myself. It took me 20 years of hard traveling to poke out those dynamic problems.

It is interesting how certain points in time become defining moments; in the way some people become your role models. After my mother's body gave up, she went blind. Dad, who hadn't been much good at nurturing her for the previous 48 years, tended her with the utmost devotion, second, by, second. He remembered the time when she used to dress up for him in satin gowns and go to balls; enroll men into her orbit with her goodness. Now, she was wrapped in a shawl and weighed less than four stone.

The second hardest decision I had yet to make. I knew that it had something to do with leaving Hennie. The intensity of making a decision is depicted in songs, and it nearly always has something to do with hearts bursting or melancholia that bordered on being mad. A few days ago she finally admitted to me that she was enjoying the drama, and at that point I decided I didn't want to become a freak in my own family show. Something had to change and I knew I had to be part of making that change. She had already worked it out. She was just waiting for me to catch her up.

Enfield Journey Bangkok, 1992

It was the same in 1992. I'd made it to Simon's place in Bangkok. The Enfield had worked well enough and would be sitting in customs at the airport, which left me with a kind of freedom you sometimes get just by jumping on and off buses with nothing to park. It was a neat little flat, was Simon's, away from the city centre. We chatted for a bit and agreed to catch up properly the following morning. He was one of my mates from the mob I hung around with in Canterbury, way back. He said I could use the phone so I reversed charged a call to Millie. The journey was going well but I was really homesick. I thought that this girl was the one for me. We'd chosen each other and she was now in someone else's bed. In my view she had taken a characteristic route towards relationship mediocrity, but I would say that wouldn't I? She ended up with someone because she was so fearful of being on her own. Interestingly, so beautiful was she that she could have had any man she chose, but instead grabbed the first one that came along. I was oddly fearful that Hennie would make the same mistake.

Then, life was for me was a bridge to cross over but on which I could never build a house. I remember the yellow waves of nausea as we spoke. This love thing, it just always got me. Always drove me mad. It always fucking blew my mind because I was always out there with no normality from which to draw reference. As we spoke I imagined how she looked. She would be wearing the usual junk cosmetics; red nails – fingers and toes – bleached blond hair and always the scarlet red lips. I remember her wearing the sort of perfume that penetrated through tobacco and liquor smells, but she carried it well in an X-rated sort of way and gave you no doubt what it was she did best. Her singsong voice would cut through your anger like a butter knife. When I was in Calcutta I knew she was in bed with someone, by Bangkok it was well over, but I persevered until Perth, and then gave up on the Stuart Highway. I tried to seduce one of her mates to come and join me and made my Dad send her a bunch of flowers. A dozen red roses were delivered post haste to her mum's house in Wilmslow but she never made it to the bus stop let alone the airport. The last I heard she was a heroin addict and her looks were beginning to fade.

After the phone call I slept. The consistent hum of Bangkok traffic never stops. In this city there is no season of sleep. No quiet sounds and bird song to gently jiggle you out of your dreams. Same traffic sounds, up you get, horns and brakes and engines accelerating and off you go again. The next night I slept in a brothel. The café owner looked after her charge and when the price was agreed I was shown a room, after which the girl followed. Outside, neon lights flashed on and off, lighting up the walls with electric blues and reds. The noise became a little quieter. Sex was very simple and gentle, it satiated not so much the carnal desires, and holding this girl in my arms, I felt less alone and hugged her safely until we fell asleep.

The next day I pulled my bike out of customs and went round a few bars with Simon and a day or so later started riding to Kuala Lumpur. It is a common belief that travelling is a step towards self-reliance, but as I blatted across the Thai landscape, I wanted it not always to be so. In my head I changed the subject to the sound of the engine, listening to the tappets ticking away and the pushing of air and resultant explosion at each turn at the top of the piston. I was amazed at the technology I only half understood. I was really ignorant of the chemistry of the power within the internal combustion engine, but like the ancients, ignorant of nature, listening and watching for signs, then, Jupiter's lightening was terrifying. I remember reciting an Old Icelandic poem called *'The Wanderer'* which I carried with me:

> *Frequently have I had to mourn alone*
> *My cares each morning; now no living man*
> *Exists to whom I dare reveal my heart openly*
> *Travel the exile's path; fate is relentless*
> *A weary heart cannot oppose inexorable fate*
> *And so those jealous of their reputation*
> *Often bind fast their sadness in their breasts.*

*

Spain, August 2004

The following morning the boys woke up breezily, with big wide smiles. They were ravenous and breakfasted on muesli, toast, eggs, ham and cheese all squashed down with floods of orange juice. If I'd known then what was to befall us in a couple of days, I should have stayed there for a week and ridden slowly back to Malaga. Instead we rode hard to Berja, an undistinguished but friendly working town a stone's throw from Almeria.

The Hostel de Gasolinera was precisely that; a hotel over a gas station. At seven euros for the boys to sleep on a mattress and for me to have my own bed it was a bargain. Once we'd washed we went downstairs for dinner. I drank beer and the boys ate tapas and chips. A couple of nice looking girls kept glancing across at me as if to say, 'how the hell did *you* produce such lovely children?' But I didn't care. My children were known as *'rubios'*, the blond ones, a rarity in dark haired Spain. In any case, I'd already undressed these bar chicks in my head and put their clothes back on. I was more concerned with working out, as a technical exercise, which had the greatest pulling power; children who looked like puppies, or a fast bike. I was a simple man. Sometimes it made sense and sometimes it didn't.

The next day we rode to Almeria. I quickly found lodgings in a beautiful tall-roomed merchant's house that had seen better days. When we all woke up, the air was full of the honking sounds that cars round here need to make in order to function. Soon we found the promenade and I made for a café and started writing my diary when Juno suddenly jumped on the promenade wall and I leaped from my table to grab him. Sweet little twerp was about to haul himself over a 6 ft drop. Grabbed, chastised, I looked around and saw that my computer had gone, the bag had been taken, the table was empty. Time away from possessions; 5 seconds. Passports gone, money gone, credit cards, keys, phone, everything. I almost howled. First thought; the thieving bastards should be butchered. Second thought; my kids and me were stranded without a single Euro. Better they steal my wallet than my children. Juno was a little *'rubio'*, and would command a high price. I saw nothing; they must have been watching me, our line of vision obscured by a tree. Cunning. For a moment there was chaos – no money, no nothing. Couldn't even make a call. So much work on that computer, days to put right, what to do next. Still, chaos. For a moment I was in mid air. Then it started up again. Someone called the police, someone else loaned me a euro, I called Ben, a friend back home to call me back and I asked him to cancel everything. He gave me Sam's friend's number in Malaga,

Isabel, who just happened to be walking through the door having just flown in from the UK. She booked me a bus ticket from Almeria to Malaga and said that Hennie was due to be there around midnight and should she call again, she could sort out our tickets home. The police arrived and escorted us with their quads. By seven we were on the bus, the boys slept and I drifted off as we were being driven along the road we'd cycled along earlier in the afternoon. Buses and chaos, where did that happen before? I remember biking in the Americas; it was day 11, Chiclayo in Peru riding to Cayambe in Ecuador. I learnt then that chaos could be controlled. I reckoned that if I followed a bus, then the bus copes with the chaos, and I only have to cope with the bus. I don't need to know what is going on ahead of the bus. I was in Peru as the border gates were closing. It was three minutes to six in the evening. I paid $10 to get out of Peru and the authorities in Ecuador just let me through. They warned me that I was crazy travelling at night. They said the roads were hazardous. They said to watch out for the bandits.

Bandits can't catch you if you're moving, especially on a fast bike. It's when you stop that the bandits get you. Between eight at night and two in the morning I followed that bus. It travelled at 70mph through the night. No clear view of the road. I hit a dog. Bump over its barrel chest. I tasted its fur through the open visor of my helmet. Missed a donkey by inches. No time to react. Dark patches of potholes scooted beneath the undercarriage and I flicked the bike from side to side. Eventually I lost the bus and motored to a halt in complete darkness, and lay down underneath the tailgate of a long wheelbase truck, and slept.

I woke up, I'd been dreaming. Back on the Via Mediterranean south of Granada I fondled my boys heads. They were fast asleep. I looked out of the window as we passed the stack of houses leading up to the castle at Almunacar. In the way that this adventure had meant us pushing the bike as much as we rode it, I was beginning to see my life from back to front, thinking about the past as much as the present. As more urban lights whisked past the coach window, I drifted off to sleep again, emotionally drained. What was I to do about sorting out the credit cards, the money and the phone and all my stuff lost in my computer? What must I do next, and thinking back seven years, back in the Americas on the journey along the Pan American Highway where I'd been riding for 60 hours with no sleep, I had the same tricky decisions to make using a similarly emotional subdued mind.

After losing the bus, I woke having slept under that truck. It was raining hard. I'd ridden 650 miles in the very mountainous terrain along the coast road, which included thick fog for 250 miles. I was only half a day behind my schedule but it felt like an month. My problem was still going to be connecting with the transport in Cartegena or Barraquilla and I'd resigned myself to missing the Thursday ferry, but it looked just then that I wouldn't make the Saturday ferry either. There was no ferry on Sunday or Monday. The Tuesday ferry still left me a small possibility to achieve the record but it left me no room for problems in Central and North America. There was a possibility to fly. I know my travel organiser was trying to arrange this but even then the flights were only on Saturdays, Sundays and Wednesdays. I didn't know what I was going to do.

I woke again. The bus to Malaga was an hour late but Isabelle and Hennie were there to greet us. We went immediately to the Ministry of the Interiour to get an 'Annuncio' which would allow us to get out of Spain and back to the UK. After grabbing some sandwiches and coffee we checked into our hotel and at two in the morning we managed to get three hours sleep.

*

Back in the UK, it took a few days to get myself organised. I ordered new credit cards, a new computer, telephone and made arrangements to get a new passport. The bikes belonging to the riders, who were traveling with me to Alaska, had now arrived in New York and customs were asking for more information. I recalled all the hotels en route, checked the flights, called the riders and generally tidied up the bits of paper on my desk.

Hennie was living at home with me but she was erratic and contrary and soon moved out. The oddest thing happens during a relationship breakdown. Someone who you thought was a friend, someone with whom you have enjoyed the ultimate personal occasions, someone who has looked into your eyes and said that they love you; that someone, as of necessity, almost overnight, becomes a stranger.

On my way to New York, Hennie dropped me off at Machynlleth railway station, and on the way I popped my divorce papers through the letterbox of my solicitor. I hoped that we'd been fair with each other and that it would go through uncontested, but you never can tell. Hennie's solicitor had just divorced her husband, who was also a solicitor, and she left him a ruined man. The influence of Hennie's solicitor might be too strong for her not to ask for more than I can give and that has the potential to ruin me too. It was very sad and after I'd said my goodbyes to my babies, I couldn't bring myself to be hugged by my wife. It was all just too much and the emotions were somehow false. Who was it that said something about old love being a nuisance? Well, now, I was just in the way and all she really wanted to do was clear the way for someone else. I didn't know it then, but already she was sleeping with another man.

Before I could get to London I had to get a train to Durham to collect my new passport. The passport office was three minutes walk from the railway station and once I collected this erstwhile document, I caught the Bournemouth train south, 15 minutes later. I felt really depressed. My immediate journeys in the US were well prepared and I was confident we'd start from New York on time, but my personal life felt like a minor human disaster. Try as I might, I couldn't snap out of it. Even though I knew someone somewhere was being decapitated by bandits that very second, I felt just then that my world was more poignantly terrible than his, because I had to start all over again.

Fiddling with my new mobile phone, I noticed that Debbie had called a couple of days ago and as I was not technologically gifted enough to retrieve my text messages, I hadn't been aware it was there. She was the one who liked riding on a motorcycle. Her debut on my R1 had been rather spectacular, but in my head I imagined a fearful conversation with little bubbles acting as notation to an unrealistic ideal.

"So, how's your boyfriend?" (Dead I'd hoped)

"Great," she said, "we're getting on *r-e-a-l-l-y* well." (Fucking bastard, I mean he's a shipping clerk)

"Oh great, that's really cool," I said (fat chance of a shag then)

"Yea, I think that this is really *THE* one!" (Divorced a year after next!)

"Do you remember that ride from Oban to John O'Groats?"

"Of course, you were cute." (aaaaarrrghh)

No, I couldn't cope with that marshmallow mountain scenario. I needed someone who was emotionally dysfunctional and unable to maintain a relationship. At least we'd have something to talk about.

As the train stopped at Coventry, my carriage lined up alongside the Pumpkin Bar and to one side of this I could see the main concourse leading through to the car park out the front. My Dad used to come and visit Hennie and me on my boat in Cropredy, and I'd pick him up at the station. By then he was nearly blind but insisted on telling me how to drive. He would get off at Coventry because he used to be a fireman there during the war. He said the happiest times of his married life was spent with his young bride when the city was being blitzed, and later, Leamington Spa. War separated families like a log-splitter, but for some, the cement of adversity kept people together. I guess the bare-knuckle experience of wondering if the next bomb was going to get you was as much drama as most people could handle.

As the sun neared the horizon I realized how long I'd been flashing past fields and poles, bridges over roads and cows like petrified trees that never seem to move. 12 hours on the train, 15 minutes in Durham.

I called Rob, my mate who sorts out my website. Electronically he was my right hand man, and was well pissed, outside his old shop in Machynlleth. Somehow he managed to talk me through the process of registering my details so I could go online when I left the UK and after fiddling with my computer for 15 minutes, there was the thump of what sounded like him slumping to the ground. The moment I put the phone down, Debbie suddenly rang.

"Hi Debbie," I slurped.

"You all right?" she said, not exactly half-heartedly, but not exactly throwing herself into the conversation.

"Yes, well, no," I said, but what did it matter, she was a girl, so that was all right.

"I'm just swapping stuff," she said, "we've split up."

"What, that bloke you said was the love of your life, it only lasted two weeks,"

"Yeah, he was a bit confused." Was he gay? I kept that to myself but she was sex on legs and I kept that to myself as well.

"Join the club." I actually said and paused, "so, do you want to go around the world now?" I was not that convincing. I just wanted her to draw closure to something I couldn't do myself.

"Highly *unlikely*," she said, emphasising the word *unlikely*, which I took to be a resounding no. She was right of course.

30,000 miles as a pillion on an R1, you'd need to be a head-banger to want to do that. Still, I mean, you do have to hang on to life with a meat hook and I reasoned that if she turned down a world trip to go and get dumped by an idiot after two weeks, well I guess she made the right decision, but how come I keep asking the wrong girl?

*

On the plane to New York, all I could think about was sex. In six months I had made love three times. If this had been a Tibetan monk living in a cave reciting the *Book of the Dead* such a feat would have taken the other monks by surprise. They would have clapped him on the back, given him an extra bowl of rice and wished him well. Reports of his sexual prowess would have spread by word of mouth from monk to monk and his reputation would have filtered to the courts of Lhasa. In comparison, Western society would regard such paucity with contempt. Worse still, I started thinking about the girls I used to know.

I remember going out with a girl who smelt like a fish. This is a recognised medical condition. Her skin smelt like cod and even though she was a tremendous girl, I couldn't get over the haddock odour when we made love. We got on well but obviously going down on her was impossible so we talked a lot instead. Just after her I went out with Linda. She had bucked teeth but possessed a body to die for. I don't know why she dumped me but it had something to do with her meeting a policeman in New York. I went out to see her but she stood me up so I flew to San Francisco and ended up in bed with a woman who worked in a bookshop in the *Grateful Dead* district of Haight. She had the most enormous breasts. They were 56 inches all the way around, and for a boy from the country, they were nuclear. So big and heavy was each breast that it took quite a heave to right them on her chest before they rolled down back onto the bed to lie next to her body. There was another fine woman who drove after me and overtook my Enfield only to pull down my pants and then take me against the bonnet of her car. It was a minor road in Pennsylvania and when I met her again in Vienna it was perhaps not the wisest choice of love adventure. I think she was the ugliest woman I have ever seen in daylight, and so as not to upset her feelings, took her back to her hotel and fucked her with my eyes closed. The sooner we started riding the better.

At Home, August 2004

A few days before I took my flight I received a call from Karina. She was one of Hennie's best friends. Karina was an actress and had modelled with Hennie in Paris. She was statuesque, *very* princessy, spoke 6 languages and was almost certainly impossible to live with. I also fancied her madly but didn't tell my wife, although I know she knew. She was also living with a guy who was, unfortunately, one of the most popular English pop stars in Germany and quite rich. I'd forgotten his name, Cornelius something or other, never seen the guy, but Karina was beautiful.

Once she came along to the house in Wales. Living in Berlin, born in Poland, educated partly in Russian and working with some of the best film directors in Germany, she was a special lady. What would she see in me, well, precisely nothing, but fuck it, the Rooster can surely look at the Ptarmigan? She told me how hard it was going out with a rock star. "He was never there, and when he was, he wasn't present." She said.

"There but not there. I know the problem," I said, sounding as if I really understood. We talked for an hour. I knew that my lifestyle made her shudder. I knew that for some it was a dream vocation and for others a social nightmare. Not the life for princesses but I knew that it interested them. Seated in their towers, waiting to let their hair down, I was just a messenger who gave them their news.

After our call I sat on the floor by the phone. I wondered to myself what it was that makes one journey. Why it is that one sacrifices everything to be on the road. Every weekend biker knows the need to go somewhere, anywhere. The moment the engine sparks into life there is a stirring in the soul that gives birth to primeval feelings. You've got to go. You don't know why. You don't care. It has something to do with the movement of your body (and your bike) through space and time. It's travelling, it's wanderlust. In the East they still preserve the once universal concept that wandering re-establishes the original harmony which once existed between man and the universe. In the West, psychiatrists, politicians, priests and dictators are forever assuring us that the wandering life is an aberrant form of neurosis, a form of unfulfilled sexual longing; a sickness that Nazi propagandists regarded endemic in Gypsies and Jews who with wandering in their genes, could find no place in a stable Reich.

I had been on the road for much of my life, a motorcyclist, a cyclist and a nomad, travelling each day into my best thoughts, knowing of no conceit so burdensome that cannot be ridden away from. The more you sit still, the more you feel ill, and yet, the poets and the writers immobilised by drink, drugs, inclination or madness, have been amongst the greatest of literary voyagers. The founders of monastic rule were forever devising techniques for quelling wanderlust in their novices, yet Christ and the Apostles walked their journeys through the hills of Palestine.

New York City 1ˢᵗ September 2004

On the Air Train out of JFK, I call Malcolm, my freighting agent in Florida to see if the bikes are through customs, but he says that they're stuck. More information is required. I am really short with him and am so pissed off. We agree to talk in the morning. Down the Van Hyke Expressway, past the shabby side of the city I sit in a cab with Elspeth and Jason. The old team is back together again. This is the fifth time I'll be taking riders around the US and the start doesn't get any easier.

In the morning Elspeth and I brief the riders. I call the freighters again and we fax more information. It's a tense wait. By eleven, I get a call from the agent and he gives me the all clear, riders can go and collect their bikes. Relief all round. Next I finalise the insurance paperwork at Mandells on Long Island. Devin and Gail have been working on this late and I transfer the money from the UK and the documents are faxed to the freighters for me to pick up later. Pat has turned up from Detroit with his mate John and the back-up van. Elspeth and Jason go ahead with Pat to sort out last minute issues with customs. I pay the hotel and jump in a cab. The Republicans are wrapping up their convention to nominate President Bush as their candidate for re-election and New York is stiff with cops. It takes an hour to get out of town. We then pick the thickest cab driver in the universe. He takes us to Newark when we should be in Elizabeth. Straight out of The Gambia into New York and he doesn't know his way around his cab let alone one of the busiest cities in the world. Everything's going well but I am tired. I get a call, its Rick, the freight handler. He says that the bikes couldn't get cleared. There was no time before the Labour weekend holiday when everything shuts down. It'll be Tuesday before they can get through. I go white. There must be something that we can do, I ask him. Rick says he'll call Malcolm in Florida, whilst I call the office in Birmingham.

Riders have already started to arrive at the depot, what the hell will I tell them if we don't get this sorted out? We pass the Newark and Essex Banking Company, a large solid looking edifice a short hop down from the City Hall, we pass drive-thru burger bars and shops that sell everything for less than a dollar and today, right now, I don't want to be here. We hit 109 south for Elizabeth looking for Dowd Avenue and then Division for the cargo handlers. It's hot, gone cloudy but at least it's dry.

When I arrive, most of the riders have left. Something's gone right. I meet Rick in his office and he said that he came to an arrangement which if am prepared to pay a bond on each bike, we can get them cleared on the way out of the US. It was just another way for the system to legally extract money from me and quite how it differed from the way third world countries operate by charging back-handers I did not know, but I didn't care, Rick, Alex, Derek and Malcolm had cracked it and we were on the road, just, and on time.

Across the USA & Mexico, September 2004

I was riding with Mark Wisbey the Christian, Peter the journalist, Martin my mate and John who was the friend of Pat's from Detroit. It was dark, and suddenly we were in open countryside on Highway 6 by Meshoppen, near Tawanda, 80 miles before our night stop at Painted Post. Suddenly we were pulled. Two unmarked police cars brought us all to a halt. A moment later three smaller police vehicles turned up and we were told not to move and stand by our bikes. For an hour we had our details taken. Not only was I doing 75 in a 35 work zone but I overtook the goddamn police car. Shit! He was really pleased with himself, this police bloke, a small man until he beefed up his little barrel chest when he looked a little bigger. When he brought out his pen he stood higher on his built up shoes.

"Documents sir! I'm good with my documents," and he chuckled.

"'Er, I haven't actually got any Officer, they were stolen in Spain last week and I haven't managed to get them replaced. Er, we have a Driver Vehicle and Licensing Centre in Swansea Sir and they are always so incredibly slow to process lost driving licenses. I'm sure you understand and...." I knew he wouldn't.

"No documents, you get arrested, Sir!" he said. I was right. Great. It was not looking a good day. Stuffed by customs, stiffed by the cops, about to be arrested and it was only day 1!

"Sir, please would you *stand* this way," he said. 'Well, ducky,' I thought, 'you'll be asking me which way I dress in a minute.'

"Certainly Officer."

When I looked away from Officer Midget, I saw Mark with his head in his hands. I went over to him. He was almost in tears, disconsolate to the point where I thought he was going to have an instant nervous breakdown. "What's the matter," I asked.

"This is the first time I've ever been in trouble," he said.

"So what's the problem?" I asked him, "something new, that's a good thing?"

"Well, I'm a Christian,"

"So, that's good for you isn't it, like you're closer to the hotline for forgiveness." He just looked at me without smiling. "I mean, God isn't looking at you, I mean why are religious people such egoists, or have I got this wrong? What is it that makes you think He's looking at you when He's got 6 billion other fuckers like you to look at, all at the same time, I mean He isn't on the internet, He doesn't do web cams right?"

"What!"

"Oh I don't mean to be rude but if there's only one God, and hardly anyone seems to agree on that, how can He, or She, for all I care, see all of us at the same time? Am I missing something, is there a quantum law here where He sees everything all the time? I mean, what was that fucking cat that disappeared when you looked at it, Shoedinger or something's Goddamn Cat thing. It's in a sealed container and you don't know if it's dead or alive until you look at it, But if it were like that, Him, just looking at us changes the experiment, and so what He *sees*, could be thought of kind of interfering with things?"

"W-w-what?"

"Are you brain-dead or what?"

"It-It-It-It's not Him," he said, "it's the other people, my friends; they'll be really c-c-cross."

"Fuck 'em," I said, "they're not here doing what you're doing. This is real life and sometimes you get caught. You done good Mark." I was beginning to sound like Robert de Niro in one of his heist movies. I was warming to the role play but poor old Mark just looked as if he wanted to die, and he covered his face once again. "No, no, it's OK, you can go on tour with this story, I can see it, *'How I Got Caught Speeding But Sought Redemption,'* village halls, small fetes. It's a winner!"

"Mr Sanders," my midget friend called me over. "Mr Sanders, could you stand by the car please?" I did as he said and he talked me through the citation. Not only was I being nicked for speeding but for overtaking him, *Lord of the Hobbits.* "$155 for speeding and $75 for the over pass, so what's that," and he wrote the two numbers down and using old arithmetic added the two numbers together. It took 30 seconds or so, because he was clearly an idiot, and I had time to nosy about his car. A Hershey bar lay next to his Marlboro Lights in a tray that also contained his files of citations. "Yep, I'm good with my documents," he said again.

After our details had been recorded and citations given out, we were taken to a local fairground where we had to withdraw cash from an ATM to pay off the on the spot fine. I was withdrawing $200 dollars and was just about to take out another

$30 when another officer came up to me and said that I didn't need to do that as I was being charged twice for the court costs. "Got you," I said to Dwarf-man, "not so good with your documents eh?" He was well taken aback.

"No son, I got you, I got your 200 bucks, you didn't get me," and I guess it was one nil to the guy who appeared in that film, *'Honey, I got Shrunk by the Kids.'*

The fairground was pretty. There was a small ferris wheel, dodgems; lots of nicely laid out stalls selling corn and trinkets, stuff from the country. Wide bottomed girls were everywhere eating candy floss. Over the way there were tractor pulls, huge dirty plumes of black smoke belching out of specially adapted chimneys over the engine. One of the officers said we could stay in if we wanted; that we wouldn't have to pay and I asked him if there was a chance of getting laid and he went quiet and said it might be better we went on our way. "Oh my Gawd, it's a biker *g-a-n-g*," someone shouted as we were being led through the fairground to the exit. Someone else shouted to Detroit John, "You're going to have to try one of them caramel apples fella?"

"You ass!" he shouted back, "I've just been busted and you think I want a fucking apple!"

After crossing the bridge into Tawonda we turned right, crawled out of town at 25 mph because I knew there was a cop car behind us and just out of the urban limits I spotted a diner that was still open. It was already ten-thirty so it was probably the last chance to get something to eat. After ordering chicken and fries I continued my conversation with Mark.

"So, do you want to get married then?"

"W-w-well, I d-do like a girl called Sandra, and I think that sh-sh-sh-sh," this one wasn't coming out,

"Wants to *shag* you?"

"N-n-no, it's not like that, sh-sh-she just likes me." The imperfection of his speech gave everything he said a certain urgency – was he going to make the sentence or not. So I threw in occasional imponderables to see when he might grind to a halt.

"Sex before marriage?"

"D-d-d-d-definitely n-n-not. No way. N-n-no, no." It is a characteristic of Mark that the more definite he is about what he wants to say, the less able he is about saying it. The fact that he never gives up is what I most admire about him, so I lobbed in yet another spanner in his rack and pinion verbal machinery.

"So you've never had sex then?"

"Er, no."

"You're not alone mate," I said, "apart from a rather sheepish shag in the summer it's been pretty barren myself,"

"Oh really?"

"Fucking disaster mate," I said, "you're definitely not alone. I bet most of the blokes on this trip don't get it as often as they say. So if you don't marry this girl, what then?"

"Well, I'll go and be a monk.. I'm g-g-going to Devon to consider becoming an Apostolate. The only thing is that I-I-I'd have to give up my bike because I'd have to take a vow of p-p-poverty."

*

The next night we stayed in a Super 8 in Port Huron where I caught Mark hanging about the receptionist who had large breasts and painted fingernails. "You're wasted being a monk, you know, my son. You do know that don't you?" And he looked at me with a big mellow grin.

*

The next morning I wanted to ride with Tim, Barry, Adrian and Mike but they were going to embark on a picturesque detour on the shore of Lake Huron and I needed to get to the hotel as soon as possible so I could link up with Elspeth in case anything more serious than a broken bike transpired. Having had to wait whilst she sorted out Peter's bike yesterday I was determined also to get in early and socialise with the riders. Highway 69 west to Flint was straight forward, plenty of mist, very little traffic. The 79 North was fast and moving well, no police and nothing to look at. Michigan, or at least this part was not becoming my favourite state. No doubt friendly enough, but friendliness is not a particularly good index as to whether something is interesting. It suggests the opposite. To say that someone is friendly is usually because there is nothing else to say. The cynical view would be that a person is friendly because he might not have the wit to be anything else. Michigan was a friendly place and I never want to go there again.

I pulled off the 69 at Vanderbilt and circled off the small Main Street until I spotted a charming and friendly looking eating-house. The tables wore plastic tablecloths; the old serving lady was very friendly. Jars of honey and assorted jams stood on nearby shelves and Venetian blinds kept out the sun. My meal of rib steak and eggs was excellent and hot after which I would have done anything to kip by the table on the floor but they might not have been so friendly. I slumped in my chair, almost too tired to think. There was a post office across the road, but as I'd already mislaid the postcards I'd intended to send to my boys, it didn't matter anymore. How I was going to get through the rest of this year I didn't yet know, but *slowly* came to mind. The old waitress changed the sign in the window from 'open' to 'closed' so I guess that was my cue to go.

The road surface was good to medium, the allowable speed high, police presence was low and both the Mackinaw and International bridges were incredible examples of structural engineering. As I crossed the International Bridge, I was high above the lake, which to the east was wide and like a sea. To the west, what looked like a smelting plant pumped out gases from several chimney stacks and different sizes of very large locks were below. The principle that you apply to the Great Lakes is that it is a sea and size wise it is larger than any lake I've ever seen. The ride into the city was straightforward, up the 17 until it reaches the Great Northern Road and squeezed between Harveys and a Dairy Queen was our hotel for the night. I got straight onto the Internet to catch up with my business. The air freighters in Sydney were ready to fix me a flight from LA via Singapore; Paolo had sent me his business plan for tours in Turkey. I emailed Matt in India with dates to receive riders so he could take them to Rajasthan, but there was nothing from home.

Jason and I went looking for the riders so we could eat with them but they disappeared into the miasma of small city life. Instead we headed back up the hill to a restaurant the hotel manager had recommended where Martin and Mark were already sitting and eating. The pretty waitress came to take our order and when you have one third of a ton of unused testosterone gagging for snippets of femininity; the balance of things gets upturned. Mark couldn't take his eyes off her and whenever she went away to collect a menu, or return with glasses of water, he would say goodbye as if he couldn't face not seeing her again. Jason physically had to stop him following her about and Jason, the boy, was talking excitedly, mostly about how various Anglo-Saxon and sexual terms translate through hidden metaphor and innuendo.

"Did you not know about something that happened a couple of summers ago?" Talking to everyone but mostly to Jason, he obviously had no idea, "I was at a show in a borrowed van?"

"No, mate, not a word." I'd been very discreet.

"So you didn't know about the 'erm incident?"

"No mate," he said.

"It wasn't all hearts and flowers you know. I mean, you

know they were a bit bi, maybe a bit like my missus sometimes thinks she might be."

"Women find it easier to think that way, don't they," he said.

Martin then piped up, "Did I tell you about that girl I was going to see on the Irish ride, she was on the other bus,"

"What bus?" said Mark.

"It's not actually a *bus*, it's a saying, *the other bus,* it means you're a bit different," Martin shook his head and Mark scratched his.

"How different?"

"She's gay,"

"Well," I said, trying to get a word in edgeways,

"Oh I-I-I see, I think, but it's the b-b-bus bit that I don't s-s-see."

I tried again. "One of the bike clubs had asked me to do a talk and a couple of girls who worked in the shop were on another *bus* but in my van,

"W-w-what are you going on about a b-b-bus now?"

"Just listen to a story you meat-head, you might learn something." I carried on. "I mean, they asked me to go for a walk around the rally site so they could have a play with each other. I was walking around for an hour and at two in the morning I had to knock on the van door to get them to let me in and they still weren't completely at it."

"That's the boy isn't it," Jason said animatedly, "we all watch Eastenders and you have a couple of lesbians in your van and you think nothing of it."

"Yeah, but…"

"No mate, you've got the life we all want, I think it's great." The waitress turned up again and Mark became fixated, everyone listened to every word she uttered and the competition to attract her personal attention was extremely high. "So," said Jason, "do you know what the term *'Spanking the Monkey,'* means, and she said that she did. "Well, that clears that up then." She said that she wanted to be a nurse, so Mark went on about his operation on a zit under his chin which got bigger because it was on his helmet strap line and must have trapped a gland. No one else wanted to share his or her gore stories to Nursey-Waitress other than Jason, who was being perhaps, a touch excitable. "So do you know what *bugger* means, 'cos this is a term we all use and wouldn't if we stopped to think about it?"

"Well my parents use it all the time," said Nursey-Waitress,

"Well, it means to enter, you know, the bottom bit,"

"Really!" and she looked quite shocked, laughed nervously and promised to tell her parents when she got home.

Mark immediately got onto the biblical definition of sex and on the walk back to the hotel, he kicked off about an angel he thought he once saw. Sodom, Gomorrah, Angels and the technically criminal act of buggering your own wife all came up in conversation by which point I managed to extricate myself to my room and start to focus on how I was going to get all the riders through an 850 mile day to Winnipeg.

*

It wasn't 850 miles but 930 miles to Winnipeg. The early birds got in at about nine in the evening, most crawled in around midnight. Everyone was surprisingly chipper and I think that they were getting the hang of what it's like being on one of my tours. Take Peter Jump for example. Former editor of Motorcycle Voyager magazine, he was writing up the story as a freelance journalist. I hadn't actually seen him write a single word but he was probably gifted with a great memory, as for photographs, this was a mind thing as well. I told him to bring only what he needed, so he brought two large side panniers, a large top box and a very large rucksack which, since New York has not been opened. At the Air India check-in desk at

Heathrow he was overheard joking that he had all sorts of knives and explosives in his bag; the sort of thing that gets you arrested. When he broke down in Michigan, Elspeth took him to Detroit, found a dealer at short notice on a Saturday and when the repair is partially fixed, he decides its fine, insists on setting off up the freeway only to break down again 30 minutes out of town. He has no mobile phone but somehow hires a tow truck to get him back to the dealer, who puts everything to one side to help him out again. He then leaves without saying thank you, to the dealer or Elspeth and when he and she get in at midnight I tear a strip off him for being so arrogant. When we leave the hotel in Sault St. Marie, everyone turns right for Winnipeg, he turns left. By the time he reaches Winnipeg, Elspeth tells me he was weaving from side to side and when he arrived at the hotel with no time for his customary cigar, he collapsed into bed.

The day itself was splendid. For the first time for a while I personally felt good. Well rested, I was riding like the wind. Everything was easy and I was relaxed. I thought about home, and early in the day I was well predisposed to what was happening, but by the end of the day, as I tire, my head deteriorates and it feels like one step away from hell.

Before I climb into bed all I can manage to write is: *The Route; lovely winding roads by lake, fauna spliced with rocky outcrops, road straightens by Thunder Bay, mist, rain, fast riding, bed by 2.46 in the morning.*

*

The following morning Mark was writing an email to the young woman he was trying to woo. "How's it going Mark," I asked,

"Oh, n-n-not bad," he said.

"Are you getting anywhere?"

"W-w-well she liked the flowers,"

"Does she think that you're a lot manlier now you're on this trip?"

"Er-er I don't th-think so, but you never know!" I imagined how it went:

Dear Sandra
I am w-w-well, I am being very g-g-good and pray every night. I hope that you l-l-like the flowers, I picked them only for you....

Outside, the lads were getting ready. Dave Marsden, Patrick and Tim, had, as usual, left an hour earlier than anyone else. This was quite a sensible strategy but far too disciplined for me. I usually start as late as possible, stop at gourmet coffee houses, arrive late and fall into bed in a heap. Yes, I know I'm the tour organiser, but the way I see it; grown-ups doing grown-up things organise themselves; I'm only there to sweep up the mess.

The previous day was hard. I had 886 miles on my clock but some said it was nearer 920. That's a hard day by anyone's riding standards especially as the second half of the journey was in the rain. At Dryden, 200 miles from Winnipeg, reports from riders at the gas station told me of 15 of the mob having been handed speeding tickets. Peter Jump was wondering if he could put his bike on the trailer but Elspeth told him no, so he rode off. A mile up the road, Martin, me and the back-up van pulled up to find Bill the boy from Belfast standing by his bike along with his mates. The wiring loom was sparking out so it was hauled onto the trailer to be transported to Winnipeg. I hate to say it, but it was a '97 BMW GS1150. This is a bike which is specifically advertised as a bike that can go around the world, and as it conked out on Day 4 of a 17 day event, that is unfortunate.

Jason shouted to Peter, having noticed a bolt embedded in his back tyre. Peter then immediately pulled it out, and, his tyre went down. Oh no! I mean, I really don't want to be rude, but where is this boy's fucking brain, in his handbag? I asked him if he had a puncture repair kit and he said he hadn't. As we were parked right by a motel I said exasperatedly that he ought to think about booking in because there was now no more space on the trailer. I like the boy a lot, but he's behaving like a dick, probably out of his depth and will do better later. Someone produced a kit, fixed it for him and he then raced off into the night. It was raining hard, the traffic was intense and the spray made driving conditions very dangerous. It was impossible to see clearly the exit points once you'd over taken a truck so you relied on the near view vision between the vehicle and the white line and you positioned yourself approximately in the middle. We were travelling at 80 to 85, sometimes 90 miles per hour. It was far too fast. I hung on, couldn't see the road surface and no one seemed aware of the possibility of moose crossing the road. Jason shot off, who I thought was going to calm things down, but instead he entered into the fray and the speed went up. And who was the culprit at the front on a damaged back tyre with a plug that could shoot out at any moment? In my mind, my head was in my heads and my heart was in my mouth. There are days and nights when this job is too hard; when the emotional responsibility is too great. One day, I am going to have to pull someone's mangled body off the highway, phone home and tell mummy that the only thing holding daddy together is his leathers.

*

The name *Canada* supposedly derives from when in 1535 the French explorer Jacques Cartier asked the Huron-Iroquois Indians the name of their country. They replied *Kanata* meaning 'village' or 'huts'. Saskatchewan comes from the Cree word meaning *'quickly flowing water'* and Manitoba means *'country of the great spirit'*. The Canadians call Manitoba *'the big sky'*; a flat strip of land that stretches away to the horizon. There were brief moments in the day when I stopped, took off my helmet and looked around. The big sky is very evident. Accentuated by the flatness of the land, the combination of these two elements is very strong, but what catapults the senses into orbit is the silence. The quietness of the Prairies is awesome. Immediately soothing, you understand the healing power of hearing nothing and staying still. For those few short moments, the huge sensory shock knocks out the need to think, and for a moment in time your jangling thoughts are bound and gagged.

Standing still in silent solitude is the antithesis of what bike riding is all about, yet it is ironic that you need a means of transport to get there, unless you walk. Unfortunately, modern day time frames make walking impracticable. Well, that's kind of an excuse. The not very secret reason for not walking is that no biker likes doing it. It's tiresome, wears out shoes and the scenery moves by far too slowly.

Manitoba passes us by as did the province of Saskatchewan and Alberta. For road warriors like us, a town like Medicine Hat was a hotel on the outskirts of town, conveniently close to somewhere to eat. The true meaning of where we were extended to a television in the centre of a room squeezed in between two Queen-size beds.

The next morning we left as usual before six-thirty. It was raining but was to brighten up later. Elspeth drove Bill's bike to Calgary and I followed. She was tiring a little so I elected to help her and once we dropped Bill off, would load my bike onto the trailer. The first dealership was large, impersonal and unimpressed with our urgent need to get Bill's bike up and running. The other BMW dealership, Aardworks, at the opposite end of town was small, incredibly friendly and they put his bike in the workshop immediately. Dave, the main man, was trained by BMW in Munich and said he always sorted out riders who are on the road. When someone rear-ended Euan McGregor in town, Dave got a call to fix his sub-frame. Within fifteen minutes, one of his mechanics was already halfway through the diagnostic testing to see where the fault lay and with luck, Bill would be back on the road by late afternoon. Carl on the other hand was having his chain changed and whilst I was confident he'd find us again, I didn't know when.

Elspeth and I shot off to tail the riders and give them support should they need it. Into Banff on Highway and then the 93, we grabbed a coffee at Lake Louise before carrying on past the Saskatchewan River Crossing, the Columbian Icefields and then on to Jasper and the Yellowhead route before hanging a left onto the 40 for Grande Cache.

The light grey road stretched for miles. The grass verge separated the road from the trees. The trees straddled ice-blue rivers. The rivers watered the lower slopes of mountains whose ridges cut into an overcast sky. On the Yellowhead we drove, hour after hour. Out here you drive all day before you get to where you want to go. In our case we drove for days. For some of the riders they will drive for weeks. For a very few others, we will drive for months before we get to journeys end. Sometimes you become aware of the notion that these motorcycle journeys are unequivocally the most extreme in the world.

We pass the blue and red flashing lights of a police car. As in a joust, we drive head-on towards trucks the size of a small street with a closing speed that would make us unrecognisable should we not miss each other by a few feet.

The daylight rapidly begins to fade, from a grey to a milky blue. Outside so much beauty surrounds me. I see mountain nature at it's most formidable. Can it not be that you absorb the quintessential form of where you are? If you exist in an ugly place do you feel harsh? If you are in an area of outstanding natural perfection does this heal the wounds you encounter in the ugly place of your head? Do we all sometimes stay awake at night and wonder amongst all the good times what it was that went wrong between the person you loved and who loved you? Do we all ask ourselves the question why it is that love, which should have lasted a lifetime, suddenly dies?

*

We cross the Athabasca River on Highway 40 to Grand Cache and Elspeth is now driving like a demon. I know she's hungry because I've stopped her eating her crisps. Charles at the Alaska Hotel has cooked all the riders a banquet and we will not arrive until midnight. Then we will drink Absinthe, and then we will sleep, then start at seven-thirty, and then ride the Alcan. Ride one of the most famous road routes in the world, the incredible Alaskan Highway.

Its past midnight and we fuel up at Grand Prairie. It is cold, close to freezing. As we leave, Elspeth receives a text from Jason informing us that it is snowing in Dawson Creek. A few hundred metres later we hit a band of snow that reduces our speed to 50mph. This is a disaster for the trip as it might mean my cancelling the section to Alaska. The weather was the same when I was last in South America.

1996 Pan American Diary
Day 1 Ushuaia to San Sebastian
I went straight to the Prefecture of Police and he signed a document that would authenticate the start of my record attempt. I had to turn around immediately because of deteriorating weather, more snow was forecast. At 2:00 p.m. I got back to the Pass de Garibaldi, where the accident happened. I followed a road maintenance truck that was spraying the route with road-salt. I followed this at 20mph

through the pass and avoided a repeat of yesterdays fall. The weather is rapidly turning bad. A cold front is proceeding in from the south. In advance of that there has been some rain today. There are flows of freezing ice in the Beagle Channel. This is only 50 miles from Cape Horn and so it is very cold. The freezing waters are aided by the lack of wind that means the water just sits there. Temperature is everything in this part of the world. I still have 2 more days and 2000 km before I will be clear of the South American winter weather system.

Outside, Charles was waiting for me as I went out through the rear of the hotel. He drove me to Wal Mart to get some yellow waterproof clothing that would make me look like a fisherman. He then drove me to the hotels where some of the lads had stayed so I could pay for the rooms, and then we went back to his garage on the outskirts of town. Wood and corrugation, tackle and chain, artist, motorist, this was his garden shed.

He said he was the treasurer of the local council, a conservative position if ever there was one, yet privately he was hugely radical. His story about how he'd driven Daisy, his white Rolls Royce, along with other motoring enthusiasts the length of the Alcan was legendary in these parts. He prided himself on giving a service to what he described as the 'lower end of the social spectrum.' His bar clientele were as rough as guts. They were a flat nosed punch drunk bunch of mis-fits who thought a fight after a few beers was part of the service. Charles served me a miniature whisky with ice. He told me how his Aunt and Uncle formed a suicide pact, and at the ages of 93, they killed themselves. He said that they didn't want to end up deteriorating any more and that their death was painless. As I'd finished my drink, he served me another one and after the forth small bottle I was no longer coherent. Everything went white and I did everything I could do to stay upright on my chair. A combination of alcohol and tiredness had turned me into a white-faced basket case and even though I could hear him, I could no longer speak.

Charles drove me back to the hotel, by which time I'd revived somewhat. I had a chat with Mark and Martin until Mark shouted out that we were on local TV. Earlier in the afternoon, a film crew had interviewed several of the riders and it was just then showing on the television in the corner overlooking the bar. A cheer went out whenever a rider appeared on the screen. "Th-th-that was great," said Mark, "I could see the b-b-back of my head," and he pointed at the TV, "that is good, b-because it is my best side anyway," and walked away with a smile.

My Dawson Creek office was upstairs in the family's private quarters in the Alaska Hotel. It was eleven-thirty at night and someone down in the bar was playing Dark Side of the Moon on a sliding guitar. The beat went through the thin floors, up the side of the walls and made my bag bounce. When I lay down on the office sofa, the music was turned up and my head began to bounce like my bag, but as I was already unconscious, it didn't matter.

The next day it was still snowing and it was worse further north. The cold temperatures were a month early and I was under pressure to make a decision about cancelling the route to Alaska. There was eight centimetres of snow at Fort St John, an hour up the road from Dawson Creek, and a second cold front had begun to cross Whitehorse. A few of us could have given it a go but it was too risky for a large group to ride in such bad conditions. At breakfast I broke the news that we would have to re-route south, probably heading for Washington State, Oregon, Utah and Colorado before heading east across Kansas to New York. There was general approval and for the rest of the day I cancelled our previous hotel arrangements and rescheduled the accommodation for the rest of the North America section. Elspeth made all the arrangements for the riders to have their bikes serviced in Seattle and Olympia whilst also preparing an inventory for new tyres.

I didn't step outside the hotel all day. I'd managed to route the Alaska riders via Yellowstone National Park to Colorado and after Salt Lake City, they would head east, as a smaller group of riders would ride with me to Death Valley and then into Mexico. It was a shame to miss the Alaskan Highway and the first time this had happened in six years. Apart from the endeavour of riding in great wilderness, this is one of the most famous routes in the world and has a tremendous history. Dawson Creek is the start of the Alaskan Highway, which is 'Mile Zero', and is also known as the 'Alcan'. In 1941, the population of Dawson Creek was less than 500, a year later once the construction of the highway started, it grew to 20 000 and has now stabilised at around 11 000. This first town north of here of real interest is Fort Nelson, an old Hudson's Bay Company Trading Post, mainly frequented by lumberjacks and oilmen. Further on are the Stone Mountains that at 4235 ft is the highest part of the Rockies in these parts, and it's also the location of Summit Lake.

The Alaskan Highway runs between Dawson Creek and Fairbanks and is 1641 miles long. Originally built for military reasons; the US Army wanted a better route into Alaska fearing the Japanese would attack the area due to it's strategic importance in World War II. This road has in fact had a much greater impact on the north of Canada than even the gold rush did in its day. Without it, oil, timber and gold mining operations would have found it that much harder to access the territory. Further on at Watson Lake, 'Signpost Forest' now exists. This is a labyrinth of home-style signposts nailed onto trees on the outskirts of town. Brought here by tourists, more than 25 000 town names now exist. A days ride north again is the town of Whitehorse, originally the site of a former settlement of tents and log cabins that served as a trading centre for those journeying to the Klondyke. A few miles from Whitehorse is the start of the Klondike Loop, which opened in 1979, and leads on to Dawson City, which was a tiny settlement until gold rush fever hit the town between 1897 and 1899. Despite being 149 miles south of the Arctic Circle, thousands of gold diggers descended on what was thought to be the richest gold fields in the world. Now, just 1500 people live there. Jack London based his book 'Call of the Wild' on the time he spent prospecting in the region.

My first group journey was in 1999 to the Top of the World Highway. This short run started on the west side of the River Yukon that flowed on the outskirts of Dawson. An unmade road, it linked the Yukon with Alaska, the Klondike Loop with the Alcan. I took 19 riders there, all on Triumph bikes and the journey represented a time when my relationship with the company was in great shape. When I completed the 'fastest man around the world' journey, the red '96 Daytona, a bike made immediately obsolete by the emergence of the T595, was only given to me because it was absurd not to. My time with Triumph was good until the end. After riding for them for five years and accruing around £250 000 worth of publicity and being indirectly responsible for tens of riders buying a Triumph because of my road testing, no one ever said thanks. It was a tremendously efficient and professional company that didn't always engage in graciousness.

I was only ever loaned bikes, never given them as most people thought and I was never paid a single penny in payment or expenses. I had my supporters in the company but the marketing department were suspicious of eccentric PR, because quite rightly, it can give bad as well as poor PR. The end of our relationship happened after I asked Jim d'Arcy, owner of Charnwood Classic Restoration, to detach his side-car from the Thunderbird I'd borrowed. I suggested he keep his chair as I had little immediate use for it. I'd just finished filming another

12 part TV series for SKY which was to be repeated several times over the next two years. His shop was located in Coalville that was only a short journey from the Triumph factory and he kindly offered to return the bike to Triumph. Jim took the time to steam clean the machine, paying particular attention in getting as much of the winter salt off the underside of the engine as was possible. The rest of the bike was immaculate, had never been dropped and no abuse other than normal wear and tear. I was immediately dumped unceremoniously with the words, "that's the last time we lend Nick Sanders a bike." And we never spoke again. For nearly five years we had been supportive of each other and perhaps that is how we should regard the relationship instead of remembering comments which have a habit of coming back to bite. A week later, Yamaha said they wanted to sign me up.

When I created that record, BIKE magazine said that I put the *'sport into motorcycle touring'*, that I'd starting a new way of thinking in how sports tourers could be used. In stark contrast to Triumph, the Mobil management invited me to lunch with the board. When I sat next to the Chairman, he said 'Nick, remember these moments of success because they don't happen very often.' How right he was.

*

The next day, the snow turned to sleet. Kenny, who had missed his flight to New York, had now left his passport at the hotel in Winnipeg. He was wondering if he should bike back to get it when a last minute call organised Fed Ex to deliver it where we going tomorrow. Now Kenny was an interesting character. Before we left for this journey, we spoke a few times on the phone, and he was always chopping down trees in the middle of the Scottish Highlands. It must have been an awfully lonely life being a lumberjack with only trees to talk to. So, when he got to Dawson Creek he clearly intended to enrich his experience. Unbeknown to me, and a few blocks down the way, some of the lads had found a strip bar, but with a difference. Having taken off all her clothes, the young lady would sit in front of the men with her legs wide open. On her belly she balanced a glass. The object of the game was to toss a quarter into the glass and the man who did this first was allowed to take a close-up photograph of her private parts. I'd never heard of this game before and mentally shook my head. Later, he sat at the bar showing the lads the photograph he had been allowed to take, on account of the fact that he was an excellent shot. "I chuck pine cones at rabbits back home," he said, "and I can square one between thur eye's nine times outta ten. I coulda gin mesen all tha' photies I wanted, but I woulda run outta film."

*

Aptly named, the Pine Cone Pass on the Peace River road to Prince George did not prove to be a difficult crossing, and I anticipated that all the riders would arrive at their hotel early in the afternoon. That morning I had a brief conversation with my wife, which quickly deteriorated as she proceeded to blame me for everything that had gone wrong with our marriage. I didn't understand how I could be blamed for everything as I was hardly there, but I sort of sat back from the whole exercise and tried to pretend it wasn't happening. What I didn't see was that it was precisely my *not* being there that created our impasse. I pretended that tomorrow, instead of wanting to nail me wholesale to a large tree, my wife actually thought of me as being a really swell guy who liked incense, goatee beards, Morris Dancers, and people in large colourful sweaters. She said that she still really loved me and then hung up the receiver and refused to talk anymore. OK, that's an improvement in relations. At least not being talked to is better than being told how you are a worthless *son-of-a-bitch* husband who's never there! I sat quietly in Charles's office, bewildered. It was all too complicated for my small emotional consciousness. A once-upon-a-time tale of happiness, now lingered in the doorway waiting for it to be slammed shut.

Meanwhile, Elspeth and Jason were working really well. Elspeth never stopped pushing to try and make the tour run more smoothly. Jason was a complete revelation and was by far the best guide we'd had on the North American journey. Eventually we all descended into Prince George and rode to our hotel on 3rd Avenue. After I finished my few little jobs, I borrowed someone's driving license and set off to colour photocopy it, so I could print my own personalised version that would get me into Mexico. Because of the theft of all my documents in Spain, I couldn't get a new driving license issued before I left the UK.

On the way back I sat on a bench near the town's Civic Centre and wrote into my diary. A couple of native Indians came and sat with me, one of them holding a bottle of liquor wrapped in a paper bag. We chatted for a while, Roy and Hector, until a lad who looked no more than 12, turned out to be 17 and was called Little Foot. When I shivered so much I couldn't reach the keypads I made my excuses and left to sit in the main library across the way.

When I got back to the hotel it was well past midnight. Carl had called and wanted me to ring back, which I did. It was a long call and he kept asking me over and over again what he would do if we didn't make the next hotel, and it took a while to reassure him that we would. The day ended at one in the morning.

Next morning we breakfasted at A & W's down the road. I sat in the van for a while and Elspeth, who had been quiet for the past two days, seemed lighter and more talkative. Dai, my bank manager from Dolgellau called me again, and we discussed my money, or lack of it, when we saw Bill standing by his bike on the roadside. We were 75 miles north of Williams Lake and I was booted out of the van and would have to ride the next 400 miles. My one day off squished because of a broken down BMW oil seal.

I stopped at Tim Horton's restaurant in the town of Williams Lake where for $1.08 you can have steeped tea in a mug the shape of a teapot. The lads have already been through, I've just met motorists that have been overtaken by them, and they are one and half hours ahead. The waitress comes over and chats, I eat, people ask me questions and I give the shortest possible answers. At 59 Mile Roadhouse I had four chicken pieces dipped in honey mustard. Nothing was happening on the highway. Everyone else was in front and I had an hour before I reached Cache Creek. Such an average day, that it reminded me how even adventurers have humdrum days.

When I got to our destination that night, the riders were waiting for me at Stuart Anderson's Black Angus Restaurant. Mark said to me that he was gutted that he had to break the law to ride each day's distance. "I mean, I was ch-ch-chased by a police car today and he gave me a ri-ri-right telling off."

Pat interjected, "the lorry driver saw you overtake and go round the right hand bend and he saw you wobbling and he braked and swerved into the hard shoulder,"

"But I was safe,"

"It was his perception certainly," said Pat.

"I d-d-did cross double yellow lines, I admit," said Mark.

"I followed you and I thought that you'd have a problem. Motorists are watching you and if you spook the driver, they call the police. They're just used to being in charge of the road and need a lot of space on their patch of road."

Paul Guy had crashed and Elspeth took him to hospital with a suspected broken collar bone. He was released two hours later. His collar bone wasn't broken but the shoulder joint had popped out but he could still ride. Richard was sitting next to me and told me how it happened. "The bike was stationary and he just fell off and rolled onto the road." Hey, it could happen to anyone! "He's very upset," I said to Elspeth about Mark.

"Why?" she asked.

"Because," Mark interrupted, "I overtook a lorry driver and made him swerve into the hard shoulder." He was clearly distressed and half an hour later he was still picking at his food.

"God would be more cross with you if you don't eat your dinner, what about all those starving Indians?" I said, "and you've been having impure thoughts, haven't you?" He looked at me as if I was a mind reader.

"H-h-how do you know?"

"I just have that gift," I said, waiting for him to respond, which he didn't. "So?"

"W-w-well, yes I have," and he nodded, before catching the attention of the waitress, "'er excuse me but is anything closed tomorrow?"

"You're just trying to keep the waitress talking aren't you?" Richard piped up.

"Yes," he said almost defiantly.

The next day, somewhere across the Cascades, south and east of Portland in Oregon, I'd ridden all day when Elspeth flagged me down; she said that one of the riders had hit a deer. Richard took a message and it ended up with someone falling off the other side of the pass. I'd just ridden across White Pass so I left my bike at a motel on the side of the road, 20 miles from Yakumi near where our hotel was. I jumped in the van and we set off. There was nothing at the summit, no broken bike but when we got to the village of Packhorse, the girl in the garage said that someone had come off at the junction of Young Avenue a mile back up the road, and that the rider was taken to hospital which was at Morton, 17 miles back towards the way we'd already driven. We both speculated about the state of the boy having head butted a major animal at speed. The bike was reportedly a write-off. We saw two riders pass us but failed to get their attention in time. I said to Elspeth that a new big problem was beginning to happen most days and she agreed.

It was raining hard and I chatted to Elspeth. What do you do? You had to step back emotionally from an accident otherwise you'd be fretful all the time. At Morton we hung a right, drove into the small main street and then turned left and quickly pulled into the hospital's parking lot. We ran into A & E and the nurse rushed us into a waiting room. They couldn't tell us anything just then but said it was Martin Lenton and that he'd broken a few bones. Martin was a friend that made it all the more shocking. Elspeth called the hotel and spoke to Adrian, one of the riders, who said that Colin and Peter were guarding his bike at the Shell garage in Packwood. She told Adrian to call them back at the call box and send them to the hotel as we'd pick it up on the way back.

In the waiting room, we waited. There was nothing to say and only the TV and the sound of machines humming to hear. Martin was a dear man on his big adventure, something he really deserved and I was very sad his adventure had ended on day 11. We would have arrived perhaps an hour after the accident so speculated he would still be in surgery. Elspeth started listening to her text messages that had been delayed because we'd been out of signal range. Peter Jump's rather dramatic message said that Martin had been helicopter lifted to Seattle, when he was clearly still here. The nurse burst through the door and said we could go and see him. We walked down the corridor and past a green door and into his small ward. He'd broken his pelvis but was stable and was going to be ambulanced to Seattle, not quite as fun as flying but I'm sure he'll get the sirens as he approaches the city. He could hardly talk and was in some shock. He made light of the incident and compared himself to a mouse falling off his bed, that it would land uninjured because it was so light. Likewise he was a light man, but he hadn't landed so well. Once we knew where he was going to be taken, we left him and drove back to Packwood, where three riders were looking after his bike and gear.

After four hours sleep I got up to meet the riders whilst Elspeth grabbed an extra hour in bed. The route today would take us south and east in readiness for when the group splits near Salt Lake City. It was dry early on but by mid afternoon, rain showers became heavier. The road alongside the Clearwater River, flowing down from Missoula, wound her way through the forest and the road hugged the bank. My bike was performing well and held the road excellently despite the water logging. The engine hummed a very pretty tune. When I gear-shifted, the clunk was precise. The elemental guidance system that routed cold steel levers into a cogged mechanism pushed the engine into a different rev range and that dictated how I might take a corner. My riding was good today, and that kind of high-lighted how easily you can ride poorly, depending on a raft of small and distracting reasons.

It was a small tragedy for Martin that he'd fallen off. For a week or so he'd be bed, bound whilst they monitored his fracture, until the surgeon decided it was sufficiently stable for him to be moved. Then he would recuperate in bed, for another week, maybe sitting up, and the doctors would assess him to see when he could fly home. The van would take his bike back to New York and I'd see him again in November. That night in Dillon, there was more news about Martin; he had also broken a bone at the base of his spine – the nursing staff speculated that another rider had hit him from behind, and this was confirmed when Pat admitted it might have been him. He was being operated on the next day. To compound matters for the worst, Mark Wisbey had hit a boulder and had buckled both wheels. He was being looked after by Jason 300 miles away. No doubt we'd see them near Salt Lake City tonight. The lads in the lobby had said, when I arrived, that we'd all ridden 640 odd miles. It had rained for half of that and the temperature fell to below eight degrees centigrade.

By morning, it was still cold and blustery. I'd spent part of the morning phoning the UK, sorting out a myriad of small problems. Hadn't spoken to my family for a while, had spoken to the 60 day world riders, hadn't spoken to any friends, never have the time. As usual, Elspeth and I were last off and I was to follow her on my bike. It was only four hours riding on the I-15 south so I could get into the next hotel and keep things running smoothly. This journey was proving to be quite hard, and to be fair to everyone, all the riders were doing exceptionally well. I was only half a step ahead of chaos, but that was enough to give an impression we knew what we were doing, and, as we were bang on schedule, there was some justification to say that we did.

*

We left Ogden early, hit the I-15 south and by the time we turned off onto the 215 belt drive west, we'd lost Bill and Pat. They simply weren't concentrating and lost sight of the rest of us. Mark Wisbey had to ride down to Salt Lake to buy two new wheels which Jason had ordered in for him, Carl Roper was riding alone and was on his own important life mission whilst Dave and the other world riders decided to take their own route to Las Vegas. By the time my little gang and me reached the Salt Flats at Bonneville, Peter the journalist discovered his chain guard had come loose and gouged a wide gash on the side of his back wheel, so he returned to Salt Lake. After a small ham and egg breakfast in the Bonneville cafe, we got up to ride to Ely another 130 miles en route to Death Valley.

*

My own state of mind was agitated. I'd paced myself well enough, riding across to the Alaskan Highway, but as it was planned I lead the riders into Mexico, without back up, I would have to be more proactive. Just before Ely, we caught up with Bill and Pat, fuelled up and then hung a left at the second stoplight and had a coffee at 'Big J's'. The lads chatted; Bill talked about his ride over an unmade track over the mountains. He was the only one to ride this route whilst everyone else took either the interstate or the 12.

Mark came up in the conversation. "We've got to get him round Mexico you know," I said to everyone at the table, "he's trying to woo his girlfriend and this is his manhood test after which she might go for it, and if he doesn't win her he's going to become a monk." It was generally agreed that he seemed too much of a biker to last long as a monk, and as I said, "he would have to sell his bike because he has to pledge a vow of poverty,"

"Not sell his bike," and one of the lads shook his head. "Losing the girl was one thing, but not riding your bike is definitely out of order." Just then Elspeth texted me to say that Mark hadn't sourced new wheels and was definitely heading back to New York. Perhaps she would be relieved and welcome him to her bosom, perhaps he will now take up orders and throw away his keys.

On the Grand Army of the Republic Highway we scooted into Death Valley along the big fast straights. We scorched round the bends and before we knew where we were, we were where we needed to be. At that moment in time we had settled for half an hour in Tonopah. The guy in the gas station handed me a leaflet, which described the place as a mining town. In May 1900, so the story goes, someone called Carl Butler went prospecting in the hills that poke out of the desert floor at the south end of Big Smoky Valley. You know the story, he chucked a stone, kicked the earth and found 10 000 tones of copper. That accounted for the metallic reds and greens in Death Valley. It was six in the afternoon and the valley was as awesome as ever, the heat was cooler but still piercing. The roads heaved up and down like a roller coaster and the bike grumbled and purred into whatever position I wanted. With little traffic on a great road, you sit on your bike and feel the bike twitching on a billion small bumps.

Just before Furnace Creek we were told to head north to Beatty because a recent flash flood had wiped out the road from the Creek to Death Valley Junction. That added another 90 minutes onto our day and we had already ridden 650 miles, but the lads were up for the adventure and we carried on our way.

On the way to the hotel I left them at the Longstreet Casino on the Nevada state line. Whilst they would be able to eat, I rode on 10 miles to check out the hotel and see if the rooms were still available, because it's a laid back kind of place. True to form there was no one there, except for Tim's KTM. A note on the door explained how several rooms had been left open for me, so that job done I took off my kit and made ready to ride.

The run to the casino was wonderful. I rode at a hundred in the sweet night air on the straightest of roads. I wanted to listen to the engine whilst moving so didn't wear my helmet, but I only heard the wind. Instead the skin on my cheeks spread to the back of my face and maybe like being in a wind tunnel, my face turned into the shape of my skull. There were no bugs in the air, no coyotes running across the road, just the thrill of riding with the night air whipping around my head. It was pure pleasure to be so close to the desert and go through nature so fast. Quicker and quicker I rode hard and could see the lights of the casino in the distance getting rapidly nearer. Yet it was an illusion, because the lights could be seen faraway for so long, that if you squinted, it almost gave you the impression you weren't actually moving at all.

The casino had slot machines an arms width from some of the tables in the restaurant. You could eat your Big Mac and pull on the machines at the same time. The big television in the corner gave you the ultimate TV dinner. The meal wasn't great but there was so much to look at you didn't even realise you were eating. Food here takes on the value of something that stretches your stomach wall until you feel full.

I ordered my first beer for a week and asked the barman about the shrimp salad. "I don't eat shrimps sir, no, they don't agree with me, no, no knowledge of shrimps at all." He had such a big Labrador dog's face, all fullness and jowly, not at all the lean mean croupier I'd expected on the Nevada state line. Outside, the air was still warm and when I had accomplished my errand, I rode back, parked the bike, had a word with Dave Marsden and the round the world lads and then walked to the side of the hotel. Here there was one small luminescent lamp which cast a slight green light that made pockets of darkness appear spooky. Windowpanes rattled and the wind kicked around the odd tin can. Further away, when that light was shielded by a building, everything was cloaked in darkness and the wind whistled around sharp edges. I lay on the road and looked up to the night sky and saw the Milky Way for the first time since being in Ait Ben Haddou in the Sahara. Compared to so many stars my problems were made slight again. I thanked God for the cosmos for it really puts us in a very small place.

That night I slept well and the following morning the lads left early for Las Vegas. I hung around the hotel, lounged on the big-stripped sofas next to the reception, bits of cracked plaster swept to the edge of the carpet. Sandra, the lady who looks after the hotel, told me that when the flash flood happened just three weeks ago, it hit a couple driving in a van. The windows were broken by the wall of water and in seconds the inside filled up with mud. They were killed and the postman who found them told Sandra that they had been 'entombed'.

Having packed, I got ready to go. I called home and talked to my little boys. Juno wants me to send him a Spider Man outfit and Willow wants a soccer kit, so it looks like that is my big task when I get to Las Vegas! Sadly I only made it to the Harley Davidson Café and got pissed on two large Margaritas. I didn't expect to stay up long but ate in the restaurant and started to discuss what we were going to do. Outside two working girls smiled and asked if I wanted some fun, but I didn't and retired early to bed.

*

It's an unusual experience riding on roads far from home, which over the years have become familiar. In 2002 on the first Moto World Challenge, Adrian and Ian set off down the 60 east to Phoenix to pick up the I 10 to Tucson, El Paso and eventually Alpine. A similar route I was planning to ride today. Then, we were to ride more than 600 miles. When I got close to Tucson I realised I'd left my credit card at the hotel and so had to ride a round trip of 300 miles to collect it. By five in the afternoon I was back where I'd started in the motel in Wickenburg and still had at least 400 more miles to do. My ride today was less eventful, but it was odd to see the hotel in Wickenburg. A sense of retrospective *deja vue* hit me quite strongly. When I reached the Gadsden Hotel in Douglas I called Martin who was upset and irritated with me. I couldn't do anything right. Poor man had just had a major operation, didn't bring medical insurance, bikes a mess, it was all going wrong for him. I felt I was throwing my life into the wind. Hennie sent me an email last night telling me she was seeing someone else. I expected it. So, I sat in the bar and had a double whisky. It was two in the morning and I just talked to the barmaid. She poured me a third and would have served me a forth but I'd never have found my bed if I'd let her. I would have spilled out my life story if she'd let me, but instead she got me pissed and that kept me quiet.

The next morning we'd left the hotel and were dealing with Mexican immigration, who, were delightful. The lads were very excited, Carl was hyperventilating, I was just organising and shepherding. The procession from immigration to the motoring department couldn't have been easier; the people could not have been friendlier. Passport stamp, vehicle permit, insurance and bosh, we're in.

We were soon on the road to Cananea and then we took a left into the hills. The back roads of Mexico are special; utterly remote until you reach a village. Either side of the road there are fine furnishings of Chihuahuan Desert Scrub and Prickly Pear. Ocotillo, so I am led to believe in my reading, whose thorn-laden stems stand bare and dead-looking, wait, *patiently* for rain.

Within a couple of hours of riding in magnificent small desert hills, Rob on his Fazer hit a small boulder and trashed his front wheel. By the time I'd arrived, Peter had been dispatched to find a van, Carl shot off because he didn't want the hassle of hanging around, big Rob had taken off the wheel and went off to try to get it fixed and I lay down on the road, my bare back against the hot tarmac which I discovered was a great way to warm tired muscles. As I looked up to the deep blue sky, I couldn't help also noticing that the desert shrubbery here had become thicker, and flowered in a dramatic valley of brown rock faces that glowed yellow as the sun began to set. The temperature of the air was, as the sky began to crimson, that time of day when the sun no longer crisped the scent. In the soft timbre of night, sweet smells began to waft over me, only too soon, to disappear.

In time, Peter returned with an English speaking man along with a pick-up truck. Big Rob had not succeeded in getting the wheel repaired and in any case, he'd discovered that the tyre was badly gored. So we made the decision to transport the bike to the small village of Banamichi, stay in a hostel and leave for Hermosillo at seven the next morning. If we find that there is a Yamaha dealer in town that has a wheel, Rob rides south, if not, he gets his bike transported back to the border and we'll see him a few days later in Texas.

After a good nights sleep my head was clearer. Instead of taking the bike to Hermosillo I discussed with the lads that they should go straight back to Nogales, cross the border and sort it out from there. I paid the driver, and Pete Jump and myself set sail for the south.

At the small town of Ures, I usually stop for coffee in the public square by the church but it was shut, so we had *café con leche* by the bus station. By the time we'd rested it had started to rain. At Hermosillo I caught Bill and Richard leaving the hotel ready to ride. There was at last a signal on my phone and Elspeth had texted me to say that the Alaskan riders had all arrived safely at the airport. Round the world rider Dave phoned me to say he was across the US border with the others and would catch us up tonight at Guamuchil. The flock was coming back to the fold. I called a friend, Mike Lewis and had a long conversation with him about Martin in hospital. He and Steve were in agreement that Martin should return to the UK as soon as possible. Elspeth said that he thought the motoring insurance was a combination package, which it wasn't. His hospital bill might exceed $30 000 and we all agreed to hold a benefit for him and help him raise the cash. He was alive. He wasn't crippled for life. He was a mate and would be looked after.

Back in my sore head, Hennie's email about her new boyfriend was beginning to bother me. That crazy fucking girl fills up my brain with so much emotional stuff. If I was an alien looking down from outer space on human beings I would have despaired, until, one day, I saw a diamond shining out at me. That's how it was for me being married to my wife. I once wrote about her that it was only necessary to have just one single person believe in you to help you believe in yourself. I remember thinking that if you failed or if the small triumphs you performed are not recognised, then you have to believe that there is still that person who thinks of you as a god and a monument.

I always believed that the really big story of your life is the one where the finest fabric of your existence is woven into someone else's fairy tale. There is also that brief moment when the *bridge of air* becomes stone for that person to walk across and touch you. There is also that moment when the stone petrifies to become brittle; it cracks, turns back to air and you fall.

*

Outside it was pissing down. Carl on his yellow Triumph would now ride with me south, so I pulled on my leathers, packed my bike, turned the key and got myself back where I needed to be, on the road. The highway was two lane widening quite often to four. It swept between distant hills to the east and the flatlands down to the sea to the west. We rode hard for a couple of hours until we reached an army checkpoint and stopped for chicken and tortillas washed down with pineapple juice. Flies marched across the table like an army sucking up scraps of meat and dogs grabbed the bones. Kids with no shoes hung around just to remind us that this is really how most of the world lives. Once again I am cast as the rich tourist on the expensive bike – which is about right.

The road was busy with trucks and buses, animal carriers passed by as did four wheel drives and pick-ups. Ahead the sky looked bright, behind, the air was full of grey blue rain. After a break of a few minutes we set off once again to ride another 200 miles.

Before long, the rains fell with an angry wind. It was as if all of the clouds tipped out their cargo at the same time. Buckets of water covered Carl and myself as we rode into the rich city of Ciudad Obregon. At the turn off to Navojoa Carl shouted to me to park by a motel and we rushed into a doorway, my boots already full of water. I pushed the door open and fell into the dining room of a coffee house.

"We stumble off the bike and into a restaurant," Carl said, "that's lucky init, and you know what, I am lucky." He paused, "I could make a fortune out of my inventions," he said.

"What, you mean your plastic egg box protecting your camera?"

"Nah, that's just one of 'em." He paused again and sat still. "I wrote a prayer for my father." I looked up.

"That's not an invention," I said, "is he dead?"

"Yea, he passed away on Mothers Day this year. He did 30 years in the Ford plant at Dagenham, nights. It wasn't that which killed him, just hard living." He was quiet for another few moments then continued, "he was a traveller as well was my dad, he drove all the way to Egypt in 1966 and I've a picture of him standing on the top of the Great Pyramid with his guide." If there is a point when small moments overshadow grand boisterous gestures, Carl had calmed sufficiently to let this happen. This boisterous man was actually quiet and poetic, yet no one on this trip would ever know that.

The rain outside abated long enough for us to think it was going to stop and then started again as we rode away. So hard was the downpour that my boots immediately filled up with water once again and I was soaked to the skin within a minute. I rode like that for a couple of hours until we both reached Navojoa whereby I checked us into a motel. The weather forecast was deteriorating and priests predicted thunderstorms and heavy rain for several days.

In the television room there was a computer so I set to work. One of the world riders was concerned about coming off in floods that had started to build in Ciudad Obregon so the rest stayed there the night. Two riders were in Tucson having sorted the tyre and wheel problem, three riders were in Guamuchil ahead of us all and Carl and I were in Navojoa.

"I love me mum me." Aw Gawd, I'd forgotten about him and he leaned over to talk again. "She's been in a home for nine months, I mean she's got Alzheimer's and she calls me with me dad's name but you know, I can't really leave her. I mean I haven't got any friends, especially in the South of England, just me mum." Carl was just beginning to relax with me and as is the way with these events, it takes time to get to know the riders. "I tell you what Nick, I tell you want, I owe my life to those Canadians for saving my life," I told him I was writing this into the diary, "oh right then, right then, put that, no write this, *'I owe my life, no…to the saviour in Medicine Hat'*." He was now well into his stride and started to dictate to me what he wanted me to write, "I owe my life to a friend, no, to Frank the saviour of Medicine Hat."

"Why did you need saving?" I asked.

"Why, because 'er," he clicked his lips, "because," and he paused, "if I told you, you wouldn't believe me, put it this way, I had an 'er like I had a divine, a divine…'er,"

"Visualization?"

"No…."

"Image?..."

"Intervention." And he beamed with satisfaction at having found the word he wanted.

"So what was the Intervention?" I asked. He wouldn't tell me and instead insisted I read what I'd written it back to him.

"My words are like a bullet," I said to him, paraphrasing what I'd thought he'd said. "I don't use many words, limited amount of communication like a bullet…" I stopped reading.

"Are you putting that?" And he cracked up, veins beginning to stand up in his neck

"So, what was the Divine Intervention?"

"I can't tell you that," and he started droning on about the climate and world meteorology, "since riding through Canada I discovered that the world….."

"Are you a world expert on the subject?" I asked, "because if you're not, I can't be arsed to listen." I was tired and it was turning into bar conversation when a group of girls walked in.

"Cor look at that!" and his jaw fell into his lap. They were nice looking girls wearing low cut tops. "I could do something with them."

"Why do you think a nice looking young Catholic girl from a good home would have anything to do with you?"

"Because I've got a lot between my legs," he said.

"You need more than that, you need something between your ears."

He went quiet for a moment. "There are loads of girls who want that,"

"Well you're doing well aren't you, I mean you haven't even got a girlfriend." A bit harsh but he was unfazed. "You've got to work hard at keeping hold of your girlfriend." For a moment I considered the sublime irony of this coming from me.

"I can't be bothered," he said.

"Fucking rest my case mate, and if you talk to them about Divine Intervention, they're going to think you're a hospital case." He changed the subject. "Your tours are really good, and that's because you've got 10 special people except for Pat. I tell you, I don't like him and he don't like me, he's too posh for me but only special people come on these tours because they're extreme, most bikers just take out their R1 for a ride and then polish it. There are only eight people on this trip that know how to ride. I mean my bike is faster than your bike, I mean I can say to everyone back home that I beat the world record holder." I was lost at this point, apart from having to constantly cajole him to keep up in the rain, I wasn't aware of his special skills. He continued to talk even though I wasn't listening and went on about religion and this and that. "Did you know what all religions point at?"

"The sun, money, MacDonald's restaurants," I replied, not looking up, "I don't know," and with the slightest hint of exasperation I told him that it was not essential in a conversation that I bother to ask *what?*

Hennie called me at six while I was still asleep. "Did you get my email?" She kept repeating it and I said that I had and I'd call her later. Of course I'd read the poxy thing, it was the message that had confirmed my having been cuckolded. Othello himself took very little convincing to believe that Desdemona cuckolded him with Cassio.

*

The next day we headed north back along the 15 to Ciudad Obregon and turned right to Hornos. There was a route across the mountains to Creel so we decided to give it a go. The sun was out, temperature about 31 degrees and the pot-holed road wound between the tree covered mesas. We shot along until the small village of Rosario were we stopped for coffee and a fish quesidillo. Across the road there was a Zapateria and next to the café there was a Telefono kiosk. It was busy enough as yellow school buses passes by, pick-ups carrying men in sombreros. Big castles of clouds drifted by and for a moment all was well with the tour. We twisted and turned for another hour, sliding on the gravel, deftly missing boulders and rocks that had fallen from adjacent cliff faces. At the small mountain village of Yecona we stopped for fuel and then a lunch of Tamales, Tacos and Birria followed by coffee. While the lads were eating I called the freighters in Los Angeles but could only leave a voice message. It was time to start thinking about the next leg around Australia.

After staying in an Inn run by an intemperate old woman, I was really cross with her for providing such a poor service. She just twittered constantly in Spanish and I began to think that she wasn't all there. She just kept asking for more *dinero*. As Tim rode off the forecourt and onto the road he accidentally rode over one of her chickens and it ran around without a head as we all left. Just before we stopped for breakfast in the town of Temochic, he then ran over a dog. Fortunately for the lucky animal his KTM Adventure has a high ground clearance and whilst the front wheel went right over him, the engine base shoved it out of the way of the back wheel and it got up and ran off.

During the Moto World Challenge in 2002 several riders commented that this route to Creel over the Sierra Madre Occidental was the most unspoilt scenic location of their trip until that point. I remember thinking that if such a day was so good, it was easy to see why a simple ride in Mexico can better much of what the great United States has to sell. It is however easy to hit on the States, but there was a charm in Mexico which it did not know how to buy. Back then, all the riders were in fantastic spirits and that morning, Bill from Scotland said that it was all just getting better and better. He was so impressed. He said this quietly, almost as an aside, in a sort of laconic Aberdeenshire way where the weather doesn't always allow you to be easy with your expressions. Equal first amongst Bill's fine sentiments was our finding the most exquisite little Mexican cricket imaginable. His back was scarlet and green with black and white speckles. His neck had a tight collar of blue. Fawn hues mixed with yellow and the whole effect shimmered in the sunshine. As he sat on a leaf overlooking the lower slopes of the Mesa he might see the crags and bluffs, each built like giant steps to give a sense of massiveness. More than that, the view was real-life prehistory. Yucca plants appear changeless across time, Creosote bushes almost completely dominates the landscape. Thorny shrubs, such as Honey Mesquite and Acacias were everywhere. And between the leaves on this bush beside the road and the bluffs faraway, the dwarf Acacia trees looked as if they had been here for ever. The wind had styled the direction to which they leaned and the impression of cleanly cropped grass around their base was simply brand new growth. For a month there had been rain every day until the last three days and everything was blooming. The time I was here before this, there was snow on the road.

*

As we were passing through Chihuahua a police motorcyclist on his Kawasaki Z1000 police bike offered us an escort across the city to put us on the right road for the border town of Ojinaga. After he returned back the way he came, we hit the road. Highway 16 took us across the desert. Long straights that could soak whatever speed you could handle. All the bikes were performing well and we cruised quickly and in a way that we all knew exactly where we were positioned. At 100 mph across the desert we had to work together. At 150mph you were out there on your own. After an hour we turned into a small restaurant. It had one small table with enough white plastic chairs to seat six people. An elderly couple served from behind the small kitchen counter and in minutes brought bean and cheese burritos and bottles of coke. The lads then started talking about each other's first ever car – Capris, Hillman California, Pat talked about a Vauxhall Cresta. This was the same as my own dad's car, which he owned when I was five. I remember sitting on his knee when he allowed me to drive. My earliest memories of him were helping me steer the car. Of all the bad memories I had as a five year old, this was the only good one.

As the group left, I hung back. I felt like riding a while by myself. There were views of the desert I didn't want to share with anyone. As you ride along the two-way road, you feel the slightly harsh surface transfer through the bike to your body. The desert is full of scrub and Honey Mesquite and from each side of the plains it stretches to a mountain range. The distant skyline, magnificently craggy, descends in a blue-grey colour to the plain that is split by a vast canyon. I was in awe of the nature. A storm had already gathered and was pouring rain. Rivulets and waterfalls spouted out of the mountainsides and the wind began to rise. I stood by the bike and for the briefest of times by myself, I just watched in silence. If anything represented the loneliness I sometimes felt, it was at times like this, when on the side of the road, I watch nature, and rather stupidly, I imagine her watching over me.

We crossed the border without any problem and started to ride to Alpine and as Highway 67 turned directly into the path of a very large electric storm, we turned back to Presidio and booked into a nice motel and had a nice lunch. Things were looking up. After many years of travelling, I have slept on the side of the road more times than I have slept in hotels, although, that balance is fortunately changing.

When we arrived at the Holland Hotel Carla was waiting for us and gave us the grand lecture about what was cool and what we should be doing in Alpine. She was one of the great characters of the world and ran the hotel with a charm that a thousand miles of charmed hotels could not beat. Riders duly installed, I booked a hotel in New York for Dave and his wife, gave big Rob on the Aprilia the task of routing us across Texas, Chris Sully and Dave would find a hotel base in Los Angeles whilst we prepared the bikes for air freighting to Sydney.

Meanwhile, Brenda, a girl I met at the Holland two years ago, kind of wanted me to get in touch so I gave her a call. She lived across the railroad tracks on the left from a road that led from the grocery store and seemed really pleased to see me. I took a bottle of wine and we chatted. Her husband had made her move from Texas to Mississippi and within three weeks of being there he moved out of the family home. He wanted to kill her and everyone else and went off his head. He was mad she married him, mad that she made him have her baby, mad that she'd left him and mad that she wouldn't have him back. Her U-Haul truck was already loaded when the divorce papers were put into her mailbox. She set off immediately and moved right back to the house where it all began. He was coming over next week and she said that sometimes she was in fear of her life. "I've thought how he might do it and I just ask that my daughter doesn't see it."

I drank my wine and was quiet for a moment. She said to me that when I brought my world riders through Alpine before, we chatted and laughed a lot. She said that we kissed briefly. I didn't remember and said I did but was sure it was just a social caress. And then she said she was in a daze for three weeks because she'd met me. She said she'd fallen in love with me and had thought about me a lot since. The answer machine rang and her boyfriend left a message ending with 'I love you'. "He's 55 and I'm 35 and I can't say that I'm ready for the responsibility of someone *l-e-r-vin'* me," she said, and then we sort of gravitated towards each other and held each other tight. It was a strong hug, a small conjoining of two little people on the road. After my hug she cocked her head backwards and laughed the way good girls do when they want to be bad and then she put her hand down the front of my trousers and said, "*w-a-y-l-l* that's kind of *m-a-g-h-t-y* fine down here *huh?*" and she grinned and then said she wouldn't *f-e-r-c-k* me but she'd let me play with her tits instead. I told her that I liked her southern Texan Baptist belt hospitality and she said, "*W-a-y-e-s-t-e-r-n.*"

"Yea, but we are south?"

"Corpus Christi is considered south," she said, "I'm *W-A-Y-S-T* Texan."

Then she kicked me out and told me to send her a postcard. I said to meet me at the Holland next time I was in town and she said that she would.

*

When we set off the next morning to Marathon I was riding alongside a truck when suddenly I started thinking about my Dad. He'd died some years ago and was my great inspiration. I said hello in my head and asked him to keep me safe, and just a few seconds later a big ginger tom cat ran uncertainly across the road. I was half a length back from the front of the truck and as the cat ran towards the truck, the truck braked, swerved a little and the cat missed the front wheels, was knocked off balance by the first trailer wheels then crushed by the back wheels. Maybe a full second earlier I would have hit it. The animal would have tensed its muscles prior to impact to maybe take both my wheels off the ground. Most likely I'd stay upright, perhaps I'd slip on the entrails. Or I'd slip under the wheels of the truck and join the cat. I stopped the bike and took off my helmet and looked around the desert. The wind was stirring and all was quiet, there was no movement apart from some tumbleweed skitting across the road. I said thanks to my Dad, put on my helmet and carried on.

I liked Alpine, felt comfortable with the calm nature of the southern Texans, although western Texans is more appropriate. Before them, ancient American hunters and gatherers roamed this area but there were no permanent settlements until the arrival of the railroad in 1882. The first Spaniard known to have passed through this area was Captain Juan Dominquez de Mendoza, who in 1683-1684 led an expedition from La Junta, near present-day Presidio, to the Nueces River of Texas, seeking trade with the Indians and the conversion of souls to the Catholic faith. In 1839, Dr. Henry Connelly, an American trader in Chihuahua City, led a caravan of wagons through this area en route to St. Louis, Missouri to purchase goods for resale in northern Mexico. That was interesting. There was also abundant water, grass, and firewood at Burgess Springs, now Kokernot Springs. The final segment of the transcontinental Southern Pacific Railroad began here in two directions in July 1881. I find railroads so fascinating, like canal culture in Britain, the railways were built by Navigators – 'Navvies' – all with the same spirit of the frontier. One segment was built eastward from El Paso and reached Alpine in 1882 whilst another segment was built westward from San Antonio. Alpine came into existence in its present location in 1882 because of the water supply essential for the operation of steam locomotives. Then a town quickly sprang up around the railroad with cafes, rooming houses, saloons, grocery stores, and merchandise establishments on both sides of the railroad tracks.

*

When I left Brenda's I headed downhill to the rail track, turned left and walked along the sleepers and stones until I was alongside the Holland. A big yellow Union Pacific engine was coupled to three other locomotives and I watched it come towards me. It's three big lights lighting the track. I said to Brenda that I loved the sound of the rail road and she said that she's never lived more than 500 yards away from a track. The haunting sound of the horn was completely woven into her home life. For me, it was also part of my home life, except that my home, was where I happened to be.

The following morning we rode across the flat pan face of Texas. Such was the almost unimaginable flatness of the landscape that it played a trick on your mind and it curved. For me, the horizon seemed to go on forever and I felt drawn to that void, which is what forever is. Forever and this flatness made me feel uneasy in a way that riding in mountains made me feel secure. Arkansas was next on the tick list, except that it wasn't really like that. The challenge of this journey was the movement across a continent, hardly huge cultural interaction and certainly not cerebral. Much of the conversation between the riders and me centered on women and beer and that didn't happen a lot because there was no time. It's possible that these people have unknowingly been experimenting with a new way of riding their bike. Not really holistic, more like a bullet that hits the consciousness of anyone who meets us. The downside is that the organization can only just keep up with this burgeoning dream, and at the seams of the way I run things, it shows.; but the best part of this journey is the simple fact that everyone who meets the lads think of them as heroes, and what value can you put on that?

*

At Palastine, I noticed a Sonic and parked in one of their ordering bays. After ordering a Philly Cheese-steak a waitress came outside to smoke a cigarette. She was pretty with the sort of animated movements you wouldn't normally associate with such a dull job. She said it was dull; she came over to my table to chat. She said she'd leave now if she could. "Come to New York, I'll give you a lift," I told her,

"Let's go," she said and then shook her head and said that she couldn't.

"Why not?" I was in my stray dog mood and would've given her a lift. She had a two-year-old son from a boyfriend who has never seen him. The boyfriend was a big mistake and she got rid of him. There was no maintenance or social funding so she had to work in a Sonic.

"I'm going to be here all my life," she said and then introduced herself as Tabby along with the name of her son who was called Dakota. "You can't do things without money and I'm stuck here." It was sad that her dreams never really got off the ground, but you could populate a continent with the young mums whose boyfriends have squandered the hope of young love.

*

When I crossed the border to Arkansas, it was the poorest state in America that I have seen. Most of the people I saw were black, certainly those I saw outside and close to the road. They were really friendly. Three women gently took the micky when I told them I was riding to New York. Cackling and touching my arm as if to make sure I was real, they roared with laughter. People who dress in one piece leather outfits on a bike that looks like mine don't pass by these parts very often, and if they do, they don't stop long. You could tell. The fantastic image kept you completely safe. Curiosity might have killed the cat, but in human life it creates a bond. People are essentially good and just need you to give them a sprig of honesty for them to relax. The tough boys were in awe, the girls fell about; the bike was the hero and being *on the road* always touched a nerve. Then a guy turned up who I immediately didn't like – the bad spanner in the toolbox - "hey boy, yer goin' ta get yerself knocked on tha *heyd* and get yerself *rayped* and you'll be pulled of tha' *motorsickle* and tha's the end of *yooo* boy." I was in a gas station and I just looked at the gas attendant.

"Don't tell him that," she said, "he doesn't need to know all about that."

"Oh yes he does and they'll jus' come an' grab him and pull him into tha' swamp and that will be it," and then he left.

"Crazy guy huh?" I said.

"Yea, he lives over the way, we call him Crazy Joe."

Outside, three heads popped out of the window of a pickup, "hey son, c'mon over here and tell us where yer from." A girl shouted me over. They were extremely odd looking. Eyes bit too far apart, strange smiles, large heads, something not quite right. I told them and they frowned and then drove off leaving me in the dark. The gas station had just closed down for the night and I could see nothing. I half expected Crazy Joe to come back and try and pull me into the swamp so got on my bike and just concentrated on the riding. It was a fast journey once I'd reached Highway 9, a lesser used Louisiana byway and I was slightly conscious of the fact that the bush came up to the edge of the road which gave me no protection should a deer dart out. The mindset squeezes out the thought before it could sit long, it had too, a large animal would destroy my bike, collapse the folks, bend the frame, twist the bars and buckle the wheels. I would fly through its stomach, and assuming I hit enough bones, would hopefully be dead before I hit the ground. The trees rushed by as a million bugs, illuminated by my lights, pelted me with their bodies, so they too could die.

Diary Greenwood Texas September 2004

By one in the morning I have found time to write. Sitting on the car park pavement I am alone. Seven 'til one-thirty on the phone, then 501 hard miles spread across Texas, Arkansas and Mississippi. At eleven o'clock at night I've arrived. Fifteen minutes later I've showered, collected my crispy chicken take-out and eaten it. It takes a little longer to be able to process what you've done in the day. Sometimes it takes all night to sort out ideas and images only for it all to get jumbled up with the next day. The sensory overload is high and very noticeable in some of the riders. For some, the dramatic content of the journey is what a journey is all about. I think about the bike as a great gift. How the pumping pistons just keep on going. How the balance of it's essential elements- engine and frame – keep me upright on the road.

The built in chaos factor in my journeys gives everyone something to do. I give jobs to the riders who seem keen on wanting to do anything, which means I can get on with other things. Big Rob had been involved in some route planning, but it was Bill who seemed very self-assured. To look at him, white hair, tall when he didn't stoop, you'd think of him as being shy and retiring. He is, but he's also a shrewd operator in his business, and like a lot of the riders who were also highly skilled at something, Bill told me more than once about my own business failings. As Richard said, that if you take the 'pat on the back', then you also have to take the 'slap across the face'. I went to bed, my face stinging.

*

Millie called. Well she didn't actually call me. I called her. I like to think she would call me from time to time, but she never did. She never called when I went out with her. I guess that if I never contacted her again I would never hear from her. She lives so much in the here and now, her idea of the future is almost childlike. We've been trying to do lunch these past ten years and so far have a vague idea that it might happen at the end of the project. "How's she doing, the wife?" and she screamed like a witch.

"Really good, we're sorting it out all fine, she's being fair and the children are really OK, they just miss me being away."

"Little *bebe's*," she said theatrically and veritably purred all over the sound of the word, "and you," with a change of mood, "what about you? How are you?" I told her that I needed five or six months to be at home and sort things out and she agreed. I said that the job was hard but I was still feeling good. That I was going to put the record attempt off for a short while. I told her I needed to see her. It was true, I did need to see her but I also wanted to touch base with my former self. The last ten years has seen me undertake a massive expansion of my travelling and I have begun to wonder what anchored *me* to the real world.

It didn't help matters when, before Vegas, Hennie had sent me an email, which read, 'I need to tell you something else, I have started seeing somebody occasionally, it is very light and he is a nice, gentle person. I don't have any expectations of this becoming a relationship; he is leaving the area soon it seems to live abroad so it is not likely to become a big story for me. Just I need to let you know because I don't want other people to know before you. I don't want secrets. This is hard for you to hear, especially as you are far away and have so much on your plate, but it is only right that you should know.'

I wanted to write: 'I don't believe it, as soon as I'm out of the house, a geezer turns up, dog on a string, lives in a forest and you move in with him!...*blah*.' But then, how can a frog make himself heard by a princess?

I should have written: 'yes, of course you were right, I was a completely self obsessed and bullish idiot and didn't give you the real attention that you needed.' Problem was, I fancied her so much I always wanted to go to bed with her. She on the other hand thought I treated her like a sex object and that I didn't know any better. When the rock star, Sting said he could make love to his wife for six hours, it took a few years of everyone thinking themselves white trash compared to his Karma Sutra, until he eventually admitted that during those six hours, it also included a restaurant meal and a trip to the cinema. Hen and I went to the cinema together rarely, living in the dark hills of mid Wales we had to make up our own entertainment. So after having gone through labour, given birth and succoured three babies in four years, she also had to put up with a delinquent husband grabbing the emotional headlines, so it was no wonder it blew her mind. In the end I wrote nothing.

*

Today I had hoped would be carefree. Tomorrow was my day off. I'd just passed Birmingham in Alabama and found a small *cul de sac* off the freeway. I phoned Elspeth to have a quick chat and start to organise her flying out to Singapore when I heard another call waiting in my earpiece. It was Patrick telling me that Richard had broken down and could I sort it. He said he was by a pancake house on highway 64 out of Chattanooga, so I set off to find him. Fat chance of that. He was nowhere to be seen when I arrived. Same oil gasket split as with the man from Northern Ireland, also on a BMW. Two days out of New York and I'll have to U-Haul him home.

That night our motel was in Robbinsville, North Carolina. After failing to find Richard I got in just before midnight. I'd hardly put my bags down when Carl barged into the room complaining that no one could understand his views about the environment. He said that they were only concerned about buying new four-wheel drive cars and cared nothing about what they pumped out. "The Chinese are better," he said, "they don't say anything do they, they meditate and *fink*. Thousands of them on the street and no one's talking, they're all *finking*." He paused. "You know the more I travel on my bike the more I realise that most people have no idea, not a clue about what it means to ride 600 miles on a bike." He talked to himself for another ten minutes and I assumed he'd then go quiet. "And then you walk up to the drive-thru window at Wendys after being on the bike all day and they won't serve you until you actually go and get your bike and actually drive it round…it's the insanity of it all that fucks me 'ed up." I didn't say anything, hoping he'd get off his bar stool, "I am going to become a fucking *ak-ti-vist*," and when he got onto the idea of going back to the horse and cart and growing his own vegetables, I *completely* stopped listening.

The next day I hired the U-Haul truck and Bill and Patrick went down to Chattanooga to pick it up. Richard would drive it back here and he and I would share the driving back to New York. I managed to salvage my day off after all. The sun was shining and I rolled up my pants, took off my shirt and thought myself a lucky man to be here. As I wrote in the *Fastest Man* diary, all these things this year are of my own choice. Then, I felt I was *'condemned to the kind of freedom where I had nothing left to lose'*, not now. I had three little babies to return to - how fast things change – but still, not achieving journeys like this would be for me like not really living. It would still be like existing in some half world, never having drunk enough of the heroism of life.

Diary Fastest Man 1997
Sometimes as I rode there were spectres in my daydreams which made me feel as if I'd left my body; stained glass images in my head as I sat on the bike like an automaton. And there were the echoing sounds of a small boy running down the alleyways of my past. Instead of seeing oncoming trucks in the dust and the savannah shrub, I would seem sometimes to be looking down from a promontory overlooking the sea, held back from falling by a tall man in a long coat. And in my mind I pictured a bridge of iron that breached the waves, and I knew that if I tried to walk across the bridge it would turn to air. It is the narcosis of having too many thoughts locked in my helmet for too long.

As I sat in the sun, various journeys came back to me, relaxed and feeling easy, one after another I began to recall them. It sometimes helped me plot my way forward by looking at the path I've already done.

Diary Pan Americana, 1996
Day 27, Laredo (USA) to Kansas City (USA)
The next thin I noticed was how fast everybody was driving. The idea of US vehicle drivers sticking to 55 miles per hour was to save gas during the petrol crises in the mid 80's. Now there are no crises. Speed limits have been raised, eradicated in Montana, and whilst here it is 70 miles per hour, everyone was driving ninety. So, I rode all afternoon until very late. I passed through the glitter of Oklahoma, the sparkly illumination of restaurants and car lots on the out skirts of town and oddly, I am as fresh as a frog croaking in the cool breeze. I feel almost high with the pleasure of riding a bike whose spirit in my mind evades capture. I hear the quiet turbines of my little jet engine. I also hear the sound of tyres humming against the tarmac of a road which is resplendently smooth. To ride a thousand miles in these conditions is no longer a chore. Not too hot, dry, with the most perfect general driving conditions. At last I have arrived at the place where I wanted this journey to be.

Diary Round The World Enfield, 1992
From the roof of my hotel I can see the length of the street and see traders spooning their wares into the pockets of passers by. Standing by a puddle there is a bird speaking to himself, his words singing in the wind. Nearby, a blade of grass, sprouting out of the concrete, bows to him. He flies in a circle, touching the water with his wings and making silver ripples. This will be his suburban courtship. Far from home the bird tries again and tells the blade of grass of things it has not seen; of the red Ibises that stand in long rows on the banks of the Nile and catch

goldfish with their beaks; of the Sphinx, who is as old as the world and lives in a desert; of the beating of drums that echo across empty quarters; of the Mountains of the Moon and Air; of people who live on floating islands in a lake high above the plains.

New York, October 1ˢᵗ 2004

I had one day off in the city so I just wondering around. The round the world riders were due to fly in later in the day and everything was arranged for them to pick up their bikes from the sea-freighters and leave New York State immediately. My day off was spent writing in the café on the top floor of Barnes and Nobles book shop by the Lincoln Centre. I always go there when I am in town. North of Columbus Circle and the Trump Tower, it is on the edge of Central Park, so allowing me a short walk in the countryside should I so choose. Across the way, Lincoln Centre itself is a mecca for young students, and the atmosphere is one of experimental learning, filmmakers and creatives. I walked across the promenade by the ornamental lake and suddenly felt very alone. Dear though my riders were to me, there was no one who could sit with me and just be quiet. My children were too young to know how to do that, and at the moment, my wife no longer wished to. The people you meet on the road are too fleeting a presence and that, as usual, left me, with me. Such loneliness I endured, and so experienced was I in dealing with it; I sadly admitted that this was what I do best.

New York to Los Angeles, October 2004

The next day we set off; Hugh Brasher, Stephen Hager, Brian Emery, Patrick Bullimore with his wife Eileen as pillion. We set off to ride across America. We only had five days to ride over 3000 miles. The first day we journeyed across Pennsylvania, West Virginia and Ohio, the next, Indiana, Missouri and Kansas and the next we docked into Salida, Colorado.

This small group had bonded extremely well and rode like the wind. We were all beginning to look out for each other and the camaraderie was extraordinarily high considering we had been together only four days. Hugh is the son of the late Chris Brasher, who paced Roger Bannister to the first sub four-minute mile and who also started the London Marathon. Hugh runs Sweatshop, his string of 25 sports stores and was riding the new BMW GS 1200. He was definitely more comfortable on his old R1. He was a very fast boy on the track but still rode his GS daringly. Brian was riding a ZX 1200 Kawasaki and lived in Essex. He was so pleased to be on this journey. Apart from family matters, this will probably be the best thing he's ever done in his life. Steve was a General Dealer, bought and sold anything. He recently bought and sold a cinema, a *'scratch'*, he called it, because like the fleapit it was, everyone came out scratching. All his family worked down the coal mine except him, they said that he wasn't intelligent enough and he was rejected. His bike was a 1200 Suzuki bandit. Patrick was on a BMW 1150 GS Adventure. He was a stockbroker, recently retired. He'd made his money and now wanted to spend some of it. Owner of 20 odd bikes, his collection was now his passion and way of life.

As we crossed the Rocky Mountains at Monarch Pass, it was cold and at the top it was snowing. We all slowed right down, especially me because my rear tyre was bald. I'd be down to the wire by Las Angeles. Once we'd descended down to Gunnison for breakfast, we had just ridden along one of the top ten most beautiful highways in America. Narrow passes widened out to the summit plains, almost an Alto-Plano with Alpine vegetation with the most iridescent Flame Trees turning as gold as the sun.

When lit from behind they were nearly translucent. Patrick made contact with a deer, so close that his front bars had been bent by the impact. It was a minor miracle that he didn't come off. By Telluride, the weather had turned cold and wet. Patrick had got left behind as he changed into his oversuit so we had a coffee until he arrived.

The town itself was delightful in a saccharine sort of way. All the wooden shuttered shops were like dolls houses and so immaculate. It was a hyper socially conscious town and it looked as if everything had its proper place. All of the people were beautiful and everything seemed to sing like a lullaby. I imagined it to be the ideal surreal location for a David Lynch movie or even an NBC soap called *'Desperate Housewives'*. In places like this that are almost too good to be true, there are malevolents behind the stage scenery that makes everything not what it seems.

After coffee we climbed over the Skyway to 13 000 feet in pouring rain. I powered on because I could see in the distance a patch of blue amidst the grey swirling mist. We all rode as one, all on our bikes as a team, only four days into a journey that will take us around the world.

For me, I had to meet another Patrick, Dave, Tim and Chris in LA. I was to fly to Sydney a day earlier than the riders in order to make preparations for their arrival. We would then ride to Melbourne and Adelaide and up the Stuart Highway that cuts Australia in half. After Australia we would ride from Singapore to Laos and back, then India with my guide Matt while I dashed back to Birmingham to make an appearance at the Bike Show. Finally we would ride to Istanbul, across Europe and home. This diary was now over and I had little more to say, except end with a quote from the *'fastest man'* book and the smell of the road in my hair:

Fastest Man Diary Stuart Highway 1997

Somewhere in the desert I stopped the bike. I had been alone all day. The wind swooped around me with whispers and caresses. The road smelled of dust and hot stones, all bathed in ancient brooding light, the kind of light you set sail in. The sun began to set and the wind calmed. I climbed up on to the bike and stood on the seat. Higher by four feet, I was suddenly in another world. Wherever I looked I could see flat plains. I imagined I could see the curvature of the earth. I looked over the acacia bushes nearest to the road, and astonishingly, another hundred million came into view. Little bushes that spotted the red clay soil in every direction for as far as could be seen. There was no sound from the engine now and I became aware of how quiet this journey could be. Serenity comes in small moments of contemplation. Everyone needs to go where they will not be disturbed, yet by simply being, they were already there. It is the great irony of rides like this that the engine both takes you to and separates you from that quiet place of reason. In a few breaths I felt perfect detachment from the world. Ignorance had given me the fearlessness to get here, but seeing such vast emptiness made me afraid, because such space highlights how few people were around. Stilled by the silence, relieved of movement, I tried for a moment of vision and the more I tried, the lonelier I felt. Yet, great sages would probably have said that if they had been given a fast bike to blow a breeze around their parchment and quills, they too would have ridden a zillion miles for a few seconds of heaven.

There was one thing left to do, actually scrape up the confidence to publish my book. It was one in the morning and I was in Sydney, still taking my riders around the world, still with Australia, South East Asia, India and Europe left to complete. I emailed Robin and asked him what he thought and he said, 'if you sign off with the inspiration to go for the record 'showing your mindset' -then I think people will be gripped by it. You have to go for it now because there may never be a tomorrow.'

If you would like to ride on one of Nick's tours, please check out his websites:

www.motochallenge.com
www.nicksanders.com